Bright, Talented, and Black

A Guide for Families of Black Gifted Learners

Joy Lawson Davis, Ed.D

Gifted
UNLIMITED

Edited by: Ramona DuBose
Interior design: The Printed Page
Cover design: Kelly Crimi

Published by
Gifted Unlimited, LLC
12340 U.S. Highway 42, No. 453
Goshen, KY 40026
www.giftedunlimitedllc.com

ISBN: 978-1-953360-06-9

Dedication

I dedicate this book to all of the children, their families, their teachers who know Black gifted children and understand how they demonstrate their gifts and talents. For my colleagues and allies around the world who work so hard to address racial discrimination, cultural blindness, and fight against others who want to maintain the status quo in our systems of teaching and learning—this book is for all of you!

On a personal level, I can never say enough about the immeasurable support of my family, including those who have joined our ancestors since the last edition—my precious Mother whose spirit is with me moment to moment, my brothers Ronald and my sister, Jeanie. This dedication also goes to my husband Arthur, two eldest sisters, Ellen and Mildred, my children—Alexis, Adrienne, and Brandon, my brilliant, creative, and energetic grandchildren—Kamal, Aniyah, Dylan, Cateleya, and Matthew, and my extended family. Where I go, you go.

My deepest desire is that this book finds its way into every library, all homes, classrooms, and hearts around the world to touch the lives of families who need to feel that they are not alone in raising their bright children, that someone understands their experience from sunrise to sunset, and that someone is willing to speak up and advocate for them every day. I also hope that this book will do its part to empower these families and to help schools build sustainable, culturally robust, rigorous programs to meet our differently gifted childrens' cognitive, social-emotional, and neurodiverse needs wherever they may exist.

Contents

Preface

Genius Child

This is a song for the genius child
Sing it softly for the song is wild
Sing it softly as ever you can—
Lest the song get out of hand
Nobody loves a genius child
Can you love an eagle, tame or wild?
Wild or tame,
Can you love a monster of frightening name?
Nobody loves a genius child.
Kill him and let his soul run wild.

—Langston Hughes, 1947

I came across this poem many years ago when I was cleaning off a bookshelf in my daughter's bedroom, and I was reminded of why I love poetry so much. The poem spoke to my heart as both a parent and an educator, and I realized that it might encourage other educators to take more seriously their job as the identifier and nurturer of Black gifted children. I began using the poem in my workshop presentations, sharing it with classroom teachers, families , school administrators, and other educators to emphasize the importance of identifying and properly educating gifted learners, especially those who may not always be recognized for their gifts.

This poem colorfully and emotionally describes the love-hate relationship that we often have with gifted children. Using the metaphors of an eagle and a monster, the poet provokes us to con sider whether we will love or despise the genius in our children. A genius himself who wrote and published poetry for more than 40 years, Langston Hughes was well-known for his work during the Harlem Renaissance, a period in the second half of the 20th century during which writers, musicians, actors, dancers, and Black intellectuals famously gathered in Harlem, New York, sharing the gifts of their work with each other and, later, with the world (Hill, 2004).

Nationwide, Black children are greatly underrepresented in gifted programs, and many potentially gifted/genius children, perhaps just like Langston Hughes, languish in classrooms every day, uncared for and underchallenged. While Black people represent approximately 17%-19% of the general population in the U.S., Black children only represent 8% of those identified and served in school gifted programs nationwide (U.S. Dept. of Education, 2018).

Parents, family members, and community members all play a vital role in the lives of these children, and this book was written to provide tools to help families, educators, and other advocates nurture, challenge, and better understand the needs of our gifted children and teens. In these pages, you will come to understand more fully how gifted education and other advanced learner programs can benefit your child. You will also learn about special issues concerning gifted children, such as underachievement and being twice exceptional (having a disability and also being gifted), as well as how to "talk the talk" of gifted education, from identification and assessment to classroom practices.

Ideas and resources in this book will open doors wide for your children and others like them—doors that before may have been only partially opened or were perhaps closed completely. It is my hope that after reading this book, you will have a better understanding of the challenges facing Black gifted children in our schools and society today, and you will learn about some of the successful programs that are making a difference for these children across the nation.

This book has been written to help you—parents, grandparents, extended family members, teachers, advocates, and friends of Black gifted children. You will need the information in this book as you raise, nurture, and guide these bright, talented children and lead them toward a positive future. It is important to note that although the specific information provided in this book is particularly relevant and directed to families of Black gifted children, it may well help families of other cultures and educators who work with gifted learners in schools around the world.

My goal in writing this book is to share with you what I've learned in more than four decades in the field of gifted education as a teacher, administrator, college professor, and scholar through my interactions with other educators and some of the leading experts in the field of gifted education. My hope is that you will use the information found within these pages to help you raise and nurture your own gifted child, and that it will help you find other "genius children" in your community so that you can share the advice and suggestions with others.

CHAPTER 1

What It Means to Be Bright, Talented, and Black

Be your own biggest fan,
Be your own biggest believer,
and put it on your back & carry the weight.

—Nipsey Hussle, 1985-2019

For generations, the Black community was discouraged from learning to read and to educate its youth. While conditions have improved somewhat since the early 1800s, we are still challenged by school conditions that withhold access and equitable educational services from Black children in general and particularly, from those who have high potential and should have access to our nation's gifted and advanced learner programs. Most recently, wide scale attacks on gifted and talented programs have led to a movement to 'eliminate' programs for the sake of equity. Gifted education advocates, scholars, and parents of culturally diverse gifted learners in particular, see this movement as an affront to the countless numbers of Black gifted children in communities nationwide. This attack suggests that to rectify the systemic racism and resulting discrimination in our nation's schools, eliminating the grouping of students by ability and abandoning gifted education models will help our schools be more racially and culturally equitable. The highest forms of discrimination are represented by rejection of the expansion of gifted programs and by their elimination altogether. These practices suggest that underrepresented populations, like Black students, cannot be gifted. It is a shrewd, but rapidly spreading bias. Affluent families who benefit the most from publicly funded gifted and advanced learner programs will always find a way to get their children what they need. What will happen in large and small districts where Black students attend school is that those who can least afford to have access to advanced programming eliminated are those who will suffer the most. A large portion of the Black community continues to depend on the nation's public schools to educate its children. Even with the increasing number of Black families homeschooling and taking advantage of private schools, most Black students continue to be educated in public schools.

According to a definition of giftedness by the National Association for Gifted Children, an estimated 10% of our nation's children and youth have exceptional ability or potential for exceptional accomplishments. This definition maintains that gifted individuals are those who demonstrate outstanding levels of aptitude (defined as an exceptional ability to reason and learn) or competence (documented performance or achievement in the top 10%) in one or more areas (National Association for Gifted Children, n.d.).

This national definition recognizes that development of ability or talent is a lifelong process, and a variety of factors can either enhance or inhibit the development and expression of abilities. This is true for all segments of the population, regardless of race, gender, geographic region, or economic circumstance. There are gifted learners in every ethnic group. Giftedness knows no boundaries of income—gifted children live in all communities across America and all around the world.

Most people know about these children; many of them grew to become productive and successful gifted adults. Remember the girl in the neighborhood who went to school, and the principal had to skip her up a couple of grades to get her in the right classroom? She had already mastered reading on her level and was reading books for middle schoolers by the time she was six years old. Later, when she left home, everybody was talking about her because she won a scholarship to an elite, out-of-state college. Last you heard; she was a published author. And remember that teenage boy who played the piano for the choirs at church and was a member of the church's young leaders club? His father worked at the chemical plant, and you learned that the boy was both interested in and very good at science and mathematics. Later, he earned a prestigious scholarship to attend a top-tier university and majored in science and mathematics. Now, he's a researcher at an international environmental company.

When you were younger, you may have been identified as gifted early in your school career, and opportunities for advanced education may have been offered, though others did not have such opportunities. Some of you may have participated in enrichment programs or gifted and advanced courses through elementary, middle, and high school. Perhaps you even attended special schools designated for high-ability or gifted learners. Others of you did not attend special schools or take advanced classes, but you and your family knew early in your life that you had high potential. This book will affirm your belief about your potential and that of your children as well as to ensure that your gifted children have access to every opportunity available that will help them fulfill their potential.

Helping young people develop their exceptional abilities will lead to many as-yet-unknown benefits from important future accomplishments, but there will be challenges along the way. Because of their high ability, gifted children and teens are often set apart from their age peers. Although they have much in common with other children and youth in their neighborhoods and schools—such as age, gender, and culture—high-ability youngsters are different from the norm in the way they think, feel, and behave. They see the world differently; they process information differently; they think differently; and they usually even talk differently. These bright, talented children need unique guidelines by which they are raised in the home, supported by the community, and taught in school.

Being Black and Gifted Is Nothing New

Educating Black gifted children and youth is not a new concept in our community. More than a century ago, in 1906, William Edward Burghardt Du Bois, Ph.D., a noted writer and civil rights leader, proposed a plan called "The Talented Tenth," which called for Black communities to work together to recognize, nurture, and provide an education designed specifically for their most intellectually talented children (Du Bois, 1903). The plan would enable these gifted young people to return to their communities to contribute to the growth and development of their neighborhoods and the advancement of the Black race.

Du Bois, a young, gifted child himself, was raised by his single mother in the predominantly White community of Great Barrington in the western part of Massachusetts. The local citizens became aware of his special abilities early, and he soon became known as the "Berkshire Prodigy." He later attended an exclusive high school, where he found himself to be one of a few Blacks in the entire school. When he was 16, Du Bois graduated valedictorian of his class and was awarded a scholarship to attend the elite Fisk University in Nashville, Tennessee. Two years later, he entered Harvard University, where, in 1895, he became the first Black graduate (Lewis, 1993).

Some people agreed with the ideas set forth in "The Talented Tenth;" others did not. Most importantly, though, Du Bois' proposal introduced the idea of providing special educational opportunities to Black gifted children, encouraging educators and leaders within the Black community to start paying more attention to these children.

Largely due to his concern for social justice and equality, Du Bois went on to become one of the co-founders (with a multiracial group of social activists) in 1909 of the National Association for the Advancement of Colored People (NAACP). He authored several books, among them the highly acclaimed *The Souls of Black Folks*, a series of essays addressing social, educational, and moral concerns of Blacks at the turn of the century. Du Bois also gave a number of very famous speeches to international audiences, almost always addressing the political, social, and educational inequalities of Black people. To publicly promote the ideas of the NAACP and to make these ideas more accessible to a wider audience, Du Bois and his colleagues began publishing *The Crisis* magazine in 1910, and it remains the official publication of the NAACP today.

While Du Bois was the first to draw attention to the intellectual gifts of Black children and share a proposal for the development of the academic talents of these students, he was not alone as a leader in the movement to examine the intellectual strengths of Black people in the early 20th century. In the 1930s, researchers Martin D. Jenkins, Ph.D., at the time a Black scholar, and Paul Witty, Ph.D., his White professor and mentor at Northwestern University, were among the first to study gifted youngsters from depressed Black neighborhoods in the Southside of Chicago. Jenkins was deeply concerned that others studying giftedness had publicly stated that high intelligence could "not be found" in children of color, particularly in Black children. As a gifted student himself, Jenkins dedicated the first few years of his scholarly life to the task of looking for Black gifted children and proving other researchers wrong (Davis, 2013).

The Case of "B"—A Gifted Negro Girl

In 1934, Jenkins and Witty published the first study of a Black gifted student. This was historic because prior to this time, Black scholars were unable to get their research published in journals that were typically not open to sharing the work of Black scholars. This research paper was a study of the evaluation of a young negro girl who lived in Chicago. This study was titled The Case of "B"—Gifted Negro Girl (Witty & Jenkins, 1935). B's measured IQ on general intelligence tests, same as used in earlier studies by Lewis Terman, was 187! Jenkins' goal was to refute the theory that Blacks were inferior in intelligence as compared to Whites (Davis, 2013).

After this first study, Jenkins continued to search among households in one of the most depressed neighborhoods in Chicago and located a group of highly intelligent youngsters. As a pioneer in this field,

Jenkins' research resulted in the first papers written about being Black and gifted in the U.S., which were later published in national journals. As a graduate student, he was the first Black student to receive a graduate fellowship from Northwestern University. Jenkins later became president of Morgan State College in Baltimore in 1948, a college for Black students.

George Herman Canady was another pioneer for gifted Blacks, this time in the field of intelligence testing of Black students. While working toward his Ph.D. from Northwestern University (which he received in 1941), Canady was the first to study the element of racial bias in intelligence testing of Black children. In his master's thesis, he suggested that the race of the examiner was of critical importance in establishing a rapport with the children being tested, and his report subsequently went on to become a classic in the field (Canady, 1936)

As a result of the work of Du Bois, Jenkins, Canady, and others, we have a long history and a great deal of information to guide our understanding of Black gifted young people. Despite the work of these early scholars and the Civil Rights Movement that followed, however, the data today show that Black children remain underrepresented in gifted programs nationwide. In fact, some scholars say that gifted classes are the most segregated in public schools (Ford, 2014). In almost every school district, Black and Hispanic students are noticeably absent from gifted education classrooms or programs. Because they are not recognized by school officials, these gifted children do not have access to programs that would challenge them and help them to fully develop their potential. Fortunately, new strategies are being developed and implemented to change the face of gifted education for all children. However, many Black gifted children are still sitting in classrooms across America being overlooked, misdiagnosed, and underserved (Coleman, Collins, Grantham, & Biddle, 2022).

Definitions of Giftedness

Coming up with a precise definition of giftedness is challenging because children can be talented in many different areas and to many different degrees. In 1972, a federal report released to Congress, called the Marland Report, publicly expressed a broader view of giftedness than had been promoted in schools prior to that time. This report defined giftedness as follows:

> *Gifted and talented children are those identified by profession-ally qualified persons who, by virtue of outstanding abilities, are capable of high performance. These are children who require differentiated educational programs and/or services beyond those normally provided by the regular school pro-gram in order to realize their contribution to self and society. Children capable of high performance include those with demonstrated achievement and/or potential ability in any of the following areas, singly or in combination:*
> - *General intellectual ability*
> - *Specific academic aptitude*
> - *Creative or productive thinking*
> - *Leadership ability*
> - *Visual and performing arts*
> - *Psychomotor ability*

This definition influenced many states across the country as they began to design and implement programs for gifted youngsters with the small amount of federal money that was offered at the time.

In 1986, Joseph Renzulli of the University of Connecticut recognized that giftedness is more than just "school smarts," and he created a new definition—one that presents giftedness as a combination of three aspects: above-average ability, creativity, and task commitment (see Figure 1). Renzulli's definition was adopted by many schools across the country to enable them to identify and provide programs for gifted learners. Renzulli's definition states that an individual with *above-average abilities* in a particular subject area should also demonstrate creativity within that area, as well as the *task commitment* required to be productive. This definition focused not only on gifted students' abilities, but also on their capacity to create new ideas and their motivation and work ethic.

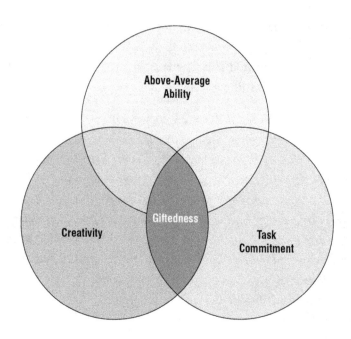

Figure 1. Renzulli's Definition of Giftedness (Renzulli, 1986)

However, it is important to understand that sometimes these capable, gifted children lack task commitment. As a result, they underachieve and are not productive, especially in school. These underachieving, gifted students need particular support and guidance in order to achieve and be successful. Chapter 2 provides advice for parents to support and assist underachieving gifted learners.

In 1993, the U.S. Department of Education issued a revised definition of giftedness based on the Marland Report of 1972:

> *Gifted children are children and youth with outstanding talent who perform or show the potential for performing at remarkably high levels of accomplishment when compared to others of their age, experience, or environment. These children and youth exhibit high performance capability in intellectual, creative, and/or artistic areas, possess an unusual leadership capacity, or excel in specific academic fields. They require services or activities not ordinarily provided by the schools.*

Outstanding talents are present in children and youth from all cultural groups, across all economic strata, and in all areas of human endeavor.

Most states and local districts have adopted this 1993 definition as a guide to developing services for all children who display characteristics of giftedness and have a need for special instruction above and beyond what is normally provided in regular classrooms. The newer definition hopefully will lead to more equitable opportunities for minority gifted children.

Gifts versus Talents

When most people talk about giftedness, they use the terms *gifted* and *talented* interchangeably. However, Francois Gagné, an expert in the field of gifted education, notes a difference between gifts and talents. According to Gagné, gifts are naturally abilities that children are born with. Talents, on the other hand, are gifts that develop over time with learning and practice. When gifted children are not challenged to strengthen and stretch their natural abilities, their talents do not fully develop. Nurturing, supporting, and stimulating these gifts are necessary if a child's ability is actually to mature into a talent (Gagné, 2003).

A child's gifts will develop into talents (or not) because of multiple influences which Gagné calls "catalysts." These catalysts include an individual's personality traits, genetics, and other physical factors, as well as environmental influences, such as the neighborhood where the child grows up, the size of the child's family, and significant events that the child experiences—for instance the death of a close family member or winning a prestigious award.

Families, of course, strongly influence the development of a child's talents. As a parent, or someone raising a gifted child, you know that what you do with your child affects her behavior and her reactions to the world. You can provide emotional support, intellectual stimulation, encouragement, reinforcement, and a place for their gifts to develop into talents over time. But parents are not the only catalysts.

Our gifted children and adolescents regularly interact with many other adults, including teachers, and of course, siblings and peers—all of whom also influence their intellectual development and thus the development of their talents.

Next to his parents, a young, gifted child's siblings will probably have the most significant impact on him. Typically, if one child in the family is gifted, then it is very likely that all of the children are gifted. It is also not uncommon to find that the parents are gifted as well. However, a whole gifted family comes with its own set of challenges—and even more so if only some family members are gifted, and others are not. For example, the firstborn in a family often gets the most attention and has the highest expectations set for him, and thus he is more likely than his siblings to be identified as gifted. Also, siblings tend to adopt roles in the family, and while the first-born may see himself as the "scholar" because of his gifted status, other children may look for different roles in an effort to carve out a unique identity in the family where they can be recognized. One may choose to become known as the "athlete," another as the "social one," etc. If parents are not alert, they can easily overlook children who are equally gifted but who underestimate their potential because they compare themselves with their siblings and seek other ways in which to excel. Occasionally, a gifted child may be unique among his or her family members or as some would say "far from the tree." When this occurs, it is even more critical that parents and guardians participate in training and read about giftedness in order to be well informed about how to advocate for and raise their uniquely gifted child.

Children who don't believe themselves to be gifted in an area generally don't strive very hard to develop those talents . Instead, they look for other areas of talent. This can be a serious loss for the child (and for society) as their strongest aptitudes may go undeveloped. Parents must resist comparing their children with one another, focusing instead on each child's individual gifts and talents, whether they duplicate each other or are quite different.

How do gifted children demonstrate their abilities?

Gifted children learn at a significantly faster pace than do other children of the same age, and as a result, beginning in early childhood, their optimal development requires different –expanded and accelerated—educational experiences. Gifted children who later become exceptionally capable as adults are among those most likely to contribute to the advancement of society and its scientific, humanistic, and social goals. In the Black community, we have many bright, creative children, but all too many of them get lost, their gifts dismissed, and ultimately undeveloped. So if some gifted children achieve while others underachieve, do most gifted children share common characteristics?

Many years of research with high-ability and high-potential children of different backgrounds have shown that gifted children, including those who are Black, do have traits in common. Observations and in-class experiences have provided us with a sound basis from which to describe what giftedness "looks like." Another excellent source of information is simply conversations with parents, grandparents, and the gifted children themselves. The characteristics listed in Table 1 match what we know about giftedness within the Black culture, as well as with gifted learners in general.

It is important to note that most gifted children will not show all the traits listed, no matter how gifted they are. Furthermore, you may see characteristics that your child displayed at an earlier age, but are no longer so obvious. However, if your child demonstrates several of the characteristics listed, then she is demonstrating behaviors that are seen in gifted children across ethnic groups and in many different settings.

You should be aware, however, that some children with exceptional aptitude may not show high achievement due to circumstances including stereotyping, implicit biases, microaggressions, poverty, racism, or other cultural barriers. Students who are gifted may have other exceptional conditions like physical or learning disabilities, or motivational or emotional problems. These children are often misunderstood and educators may focus more attention on perceived deficits and little or no attention on the child's strengths. Later, more detail is provided about how to address the needs of these students who are called " 2e twice exceptional" or "3e, thrice exceptional"—gifted, culturally diverse with other exceptional conditions (Davis & Robinson, 2018).

Also keep in mind that while your gifted child may at times seem mature or "wise for his age," he is still a child who needs the guidance of parents and other adults. In fact, for many gifted children, development of judgment lags behind intellect. As ure your young child appears to be. Remember, you are your child's first teacher and the nurturer of his gifts. You need to be aware of how challenging his life may be at times. Being gifted is not always embraced by the general public—or even by schools—and expectations of outward performance too often control how the world views and treats gifted children. Your support and guidance are vital to your child's development and the assurance of a positive future.

Table 1. Characteristics of Gifted Children

Characteristic*	How the trait may be expressed in the home, community, and/or school
Verbally precocious	Talks early; uses full sentences sooner than others; enjoys using big words; reads early; tells long stories; likes to dramatize; is an avid reader; demonstrates superior oral skills; may imitate speakers; likes poetry; writes lyrics for songs; uses lots of details in descriptions, understands nuances in language and how to use language to negotiate, cajole and convince others to believe in their ideas (charismatic)
Reasons well	Goes beyond the surface to probe deeper and discover new information; figures things out more quickly than age peers; enjoys problem solving (word, number, or circumstance problems); engages in conversation with adults and older children easily; sounds like he or she has "been here before; "demonstrates 'wisdom'; makes connections between seemingly unlike objects, ideas, places, things

Expresses self-determination and drive	Sets own goals and possesses internal motivation to accomplish them; goals may conflict with adult demands; internally driven to do what he or she believes is important and necessary; needs little encouragement to work on projects and activities of great interest
Rapidly learns new information	Needs only two or three repetitions to learn new material; puts thoughts, ideas, words, answers together quickly; may get frustrated with constant repetition of information in school or in conversations at home; demonstrates an advanced memory for details
Unusually sensitive to the needs of others	Demonstrates a strong sense of justice and expresses it early; expresses concern for others being treated unfairly in home environment, neighborhood, or around the world (this may be related to the needs of humans and other living things)
Perfectionistic	Wants to get everything right; sets and maintains unusually high standards for self in speech and work; takes on multiple projects at once
Enhanced visual-spatial skills	Outstanding sense of spatial relationships; observant; exhibits creative expression; often excels at pre-engineering activities/tasks at school; enjoys constructing/building in 3-D form; enjoys geometrical problems and strategic board games such as chess
Resilient	Demonstrates ability to "bounce back" after challenging experiences in life; shows an unusual strength when faced with obstacles, difficulties, or barriers to achievement; is described as "feisty" and "tough" by others

Imaginative, creative	May have one or more imaginary friends; tells long, elaborate stories about imaginary friends; takes basic objects and materials and creates new products; makes good use of what is available; creates unique but practical responses to problems

Davis, J.L. (2010). *Bright, Talented & Black: A guide for Families of African American Gifted Learners.* Great Potential Press

Scenario #1: *Dylan was in the first grade at a public school in his community. He was very observant, talkative, and loved school. Sometimes on the weekends, he had an opportunity to visit his Nana. She always asked probing questions about what was happening in school, if he had any new friends, or if he was learning something new. During one conversation, Dylan told his grandmother that there was a fiction/non-fiction boy in his class. Very puzzled by his use of the term, she asked what he meant. He responded by saying that the boy was usually misbehaving in class, but if the teacher caught him, he would pretend to be a good boy. Stunned, his grandmother asked why he called him "fiction/non-fiction." Dylan clearly explained that the boy was really not a good boy but he pretended to be good when the teacher was watching him and that he had learned what "fiction/non-fiction" meant when they visited the library earlier that week. Fiction meaning not true—non-fiction meaning true. So in Dylan's view, his classmate was a fiction/non-fiction person! Lesson learned: pay attention to the stories, descriptions, connections that students make between seemingly non-connected concepts/ideas/situations. In this case, Dylan's insight was very mature and enabled him to make a connection between what he learned in the library and his classmate's behavior. Gifted children see the world differently, if you talk with them and watch how they interact with others you may discover a child who has great potential and insight far beyond their years.*

Nurturing Your Child's Strengths

As you examined the list of characteristics of gifted children, you probably noted behaviors that you've seen in your child. What next? If your child is an early and rapid learner, simply watch to see how she develops over time, and encourage her curiosity and desire to learn. Support her interests and strengths by answering questions and providing resources and opportunities for more learning.

Do you notice your child creating orderly rows of blocks or other toys, pairing them up by color or size? Does he experiment with musical instruments, playing rhythms in a certain pattern or sounding out familiar tunes? When reading or having a discussion with others, does your child appear as if he's on stage, taking a bow, understanding that he has done a great job? Reading aloud and participating in creative drama/theatre may give your child opportunities to express himself by taking on the role of other characters. Does she love to dance and challenge herself physically? If so, keep your eye on this child; blocks and building may predict a budding mathematician, and experimentation with rhythm and dance may hint to an up-and-coming actor, musician, or dancer.

Many gifted children display the same inclinations or strengths over a long period of time. However, some gifted children demonstrate certain traits for a few months, such as being avid readers, and then they change and no longer even touch books—as a matter of fact, they would prefer to do anything except read. These children may just be exploring their world; let their interests lead the way. Gifted children are naturally curious and want to know more about the world around them. To do this, they may change their areas of interest many times during their developmental years. While they are exploring their interests, find reading materials of interest, read to them, model reading and ensure that they are keeping pace with their earlier reading abilities by making reading a regular part of their routine at home.

As children enter pre-adolescence, they begin to show more stability in their personality traits, and their strengths become more obvious.

However, many of these children's strongest characteristics are evident when they are young. For example:

Perhaps your daughter is extra-sensitive and responds to the emotions of others or the needs of animals, the elderly, or other vulnerable humans. Your child is now a teenager, but you recall noticing those same sensitivities when she was just a toddler. She currently volunteers at the local shelter for the homeless, and she always has ideas as to how the entire family and neighborhood can do a better job of reaching out to others.

You can remember your son writing on every notepad or sheet of paper he could find in the house or the car, jotting down notes, and then spending hours alone in his room writing stories and poetry. As a middle schooler, he is now involved in a Young Writer's Club and has published some of his short stories. His goal is to become a journalist.

When she was young, your daughter organized a peaceful protest at school to convince the school board to fund a new gym, and now, years later, she is a very successful marketing representative for a Fortune 500 company.

It is a good idea to involve your gifted children in specific activities— such as after-school sports, music lessons, chess, Scouts, Boys and Girls Clubs, church, or YMCA activities, volunteerism—as you guide them toward their full development. Involvement in these kinds of activities gives your children more exposure to exciting ideas, interesting people, and potential new friends and interests, while also keeping them active and engaged in learning rather than spending too much time occupied with their technology 'games' or being idle for long periods of time.

As a parent of a Black gifted learner, finding and gaining access to resources and services that are available within the larger culture will be one of your greatest challenges. The remaining chapters in this book provide advice for breaking down some of the barriers to resources and services, while also being attentive to your child's intellectual and social-emotional needs throughout his or her developmental years.

You—parents and other extended family members—need to observe and, through your personal relationships, value your children's abilities and internal strengths within the home and community. Your relationship with your children is the most important thing that you have, and as a parent, you are the one who will have the most influence on their future. Your attention to their unique gifts and talents will make all the difference in their level of success in the years to come.

Raising gifted children can be challenging. On one hand, it is a sheer pleasure to observe their minds ticking, to enjoy their creative products, and to relish and take pride in the praise and awards they may earn from their accomplishments. On the other, dealing with the intensity of their emotions, their constant questioning, their contradictory behavior, their sensitivities to the world around them, and the world's mixed feelings about gifted children—Black gifted children—may sometimes seem like more than you can bear. An additional challenge for Black families is providing their children with the support and courage needed to be able to coexist with peers of all races and yet also maintain a sense of pride in themselves and their own culture. The chapters ahead offer advice and practical suggestions to address these concerns.

Highly, Profoundly Gifted & Black: there are more of us than you may know

According to psychometricians who measure intelligence, highly gifted or genius range students have the potential to score at the range of 130 and above on IQ tests (Ruf, 2009). Some traits of profoundly gifted students include:

- ○ Ability to comprehend material several grade levels above their age peers

- ○ Surprising emotional depth and sensitivity at a young age

- ○ Strong sense of curiosity

- ○ Enthusiastic about unique interests and topics

○ Quirky or mature sense of humor

○ Creative problem-solving and imaginative expression

○ Absorbs information quickly with few repetitions needed

○ Self-aware, socially aware, and aware of global issues

(This list appears in a blog post by the Davidson Academy website dated July 14, 2021)

Historically, as mentioned in earlier in this chapter, the first study of giftedness that was recorded of a highly gifted/genius range Black student was documented in *The Case of "B"—A Gifted Negro Girl* (Witty & Jenkins, 1935). After the initial publication of this historical study, Martin D. Jenkins continued to search for gifted children in the Black community and administered a full range of psychological tests to those he located in Chicago and later in Washington DC. It was Jenkins' belief that there were more Black students who had the capacity to score in this high range than had been previously indicated in research studies. It was Jenkins' work that set the foundation for many scholars who also believed that giftedness or genius capacity existed, not only among the White or majority population, but among the Black and other minority populations as well (Jenkins, 1936).

Highly gifted students demonstrate their capabilities in academics, arts, athletics, science, mathematics, technology, humanities, and social justice/leadership domains.

In conversations over the years with Black parents of highly gifted students, they have shared many challenges that they have experienced with public schools paying attention to and appropriately meeting the needs of their gifted children. Some have spoken about meetings where their statements about their highly gifted students were discounted by school personnel. Others have had to spend their own funds to have private psychological testing done to 'prove' their children's capabilities. In one situation, a highly gifted student was accused of plagiarism by his teacher and the parents had to appeal a decision to fail the student. Though the school administration was not happy with the parents, they allowed the appeal and determined that the student had not cheated or plagiarized his report. The highly gifted

Black male student was then given the grade he earned. Sadly, Black gifted children in schools across the nation suffer from discrimination, stereotyping, and underestimation by school personnel. With strong parents as advocates the conditions can be corrected.

This section features interviews with the parents of highly gifted Black students with varied educational experiences. What follows are the responses to questions from parents of two highly gifted children and one response from an older highly gifted student who, in 2022, was the youngest Black female to complete law school in our nation.

From the mother of Bellen

When did you first discover that there was something different about your highly gifted daughter?
We have a video of Bellen at 4 months old quite distinctly saying the word, "Off." We were so wrapped up in the fun of placing shades on her, that we didn't even notice. But when she was about 4 years old, she came across the video and said, "Hey! I asked you all to take those shades off!" But despite that miss, we always found her to be especially alert, self-motivated, and intentional. By the age of 2, she began to read and increasingly loved the independence that reading afforded her.

What was she like as a toddler?
One thing I always found of interest was just how much she enjoyed playing and exploring—on her own and without prompting. As early as 1 year old, I can remember Bellen spending time alone in her playroom with anything from books to dolls (mostly dolls!), kitchen sets, puzzles, you name it. She was as content as anyone I've ever seen and would spend hours (as much time as she could muster) in her playroom just exploring and creating.

What kinds of toys did she play with?
Her favorites were always dolls and various toys where she could add-on or adjust such as doll houses, kitchen sets, miniature models,

etc. She enjoyed puzzles sometimes but not as much as realistic pieces that represented the real world, i.e. miniature people, pets, food, etc.

How about her sleep habits?
She's always been an especially early riser. She wasn't the best sleeper as an infant (woke up often to nurse) but now is typically asleep within a couple of minutes of hitting the pillow.

When did she first learn to talk and begin to read?
She began to walk at 9 months; said her first word at 3 months; and read at 2 years old.

Who are some of the people in your support system?
Her brothers and parents.

What are your daughter's favorite subjects in school and her hobbies?
English, writing, and math. Her hobbies are creative writing and dance.

What are three of the greatest challenges of raising a highly gifted Black female?
The greatest challenge is ensuring that she is able to always exist authentically, which includes simply being a child. Another is helping others to understand the ongoing need for appropriate rigor. A third is ensuring that her voice and her needs drive her journey and that we are not persuaded by our own or others' ideals.

What advice do you have for parents of other highly gifted Black students?
Trust the cues your child provides. And you are your child's best advocate. There have been many times when we would advocate largely based on our own instinct. And now, in hindsight, I'm so relieved we did.

Update on Bellen:
Bellen Woodard is the beloved bright light, trailblazing CEO, and award-winning children's book author who launched Bellen's More

than Peach® Project in spring 2019 when she was just 8 years old. The pioneer of the first multicultural crayon art-brand, More than Peach, & World's 1st Crayon Activist®, Bellen has transformed an entire industry with a first-of-its-kind, innovative project and art brand that has become a global movement centering empathy, creativity, and youth leadership. It began when she was able to change the language around "skin color" in her own classroom. Since its launch in spring 2019, More than Peach is credited with both growing classrooms and transforming the crayon industry and others as Bellen has redefined "flesh/nude/skin-color" in the arts as she continues making history! Seeking more inclusivity and wanting to grow youth leadership, her innovative brand is indeed changing the world...one crayon at a time! Her project has become an international movement and she, a leader in product inclusion—influencing even the biggest brand to follow. Bellen's products inspire across cultures and generations like no other, quickly becoming a classroom and family favorite in their ability to connect with people of all ages, backgrounds, and abilities. Her mission: "Created by a kid...so no kid is 'disincluded'." The incipient goal of Bellen's More than Peach Project—to place multicultural crayons in the hands of all students to increase empathy, creativity, and leadership—has been credited with compassionate change around the globe.

Questions answered by Caleb's mother

When did you first discover that there was something different about your highly gifted son?

Although, you'd be hard pressed to find a parent, especially a mother who doesn't believe that their precious baby is special, I am going to be the example around which the cliché was created. Believe it or not, I noticed almost immediately that there was something different about my profoundly gifted son. At only a few weeks old, Caleb would track me and my husband as we walked through the room. This is a developmental milestone that does not normally occur that early. He also babbled very early. It was a signal to me that he was ready to learn. As soon as he was able to sit up (which was at about four months old) I began to teach him sign language so that he could communicate his needs, desires, and frustrations instead of crying. I'd also spend about 10 minutes a day associating the words he was learning to sign with phonic sounds and flash cards. As a result, by six months old he was signing back and beginning to read. I vividly remember showing Caleb flash cards with a series of words like "milk," "water," "eat," "happy," etc., and signing it. Caleb would grab the cards with the words I'd say or sign. He was no older than nine months old. My husband didn't believe me at first, but came around quickly once he saw Caleb in action. He just grasped new concepts quickly. Anything I'd teach him, he'd get right away, and his knowledge base extended beyond reading to geography, math and science. Eventually, we started to record it and put it on YouTube, because we didn't think anyone else would believe us unless there was proof.

What was he like as a toddler? What kinds of toys did he play with? How about his sleep habits? When did he first learn to talk and begin to read?
The ability to read is foundational. Since Caleb was able to read well before his first birthday, as a toddler he was very advanced. For example, at two and a half years old, the private school he attended for daycare was actually a school and the principal of the preschool would walk him from his class to 1st Grade during math and reading. He still remembers how much bigger the kids were in his eyes.

We had him on a routine when he was a toddler, so he got very used to the routine. He'd wake up, brush his teeth, eat breakfast, spend a few minutes learning then we'd be off to our activity of the day. Sometimes it was off to the zoo, or the Museum of Puppetry Arts, or the High Museum, the park or one of the Fernbank Museums. Next was lunch time followed by nap time. He'd have an afternoon snack, read a little more, play with Daddy and eat dinner. By 7pm it was bath, book, and bed. Most of those elements had to be there in a day or there was a problem. It was a blessing and a curse especially him being in bed by 7:30pm. One time when his grandmother was visiting, we got stuck in traffic far from home and stopped at a restaurant to eat. He was inconsolable, all he wanted was his bed! When he got a little older, he would tell us it is time for him to go to bed. Now, as a preteen, unfortunately that is no longer the case, but it sure was nice while it lasted.

Who are some of the people in your support system?
I read an analogy in a book comparing a healthy network of friends to the redwood forests of sequoia trees in Northern California. The tallest sequoias reach upwards of 250 feet high, however, their root system only goes four feet deep. What allows these trees to live hundreds of years and grow so high is not the depth of the roots, but rather the interconnectedness as the roots grow outwards anchoring each other together. That is how I feel about our support system.

Most of our extended family are outside of Georgia and even outside of the United States. Caleb has grandparents who serve many functions, from spoiling him to keeping him grounded, especially his grandmothers. His Nanna brings him books, puzzles and gifts from his aunt and cousin in Canada. His Grandma cooks his favorite Haitian dishes from griot, to *du riz colle* to legumes with her signature crab. She also puts the fear of God in him with a look or a warning. My sister and her husband are favorite aunt and uncle and they only live an hour away, and they have been a Godsend in too many ways to count. My brothers and sisters, my husband's sister and our cousins have all offered reassurance, advice (solicited and unsolicited), gifts and prayers. Even their amazement has sometimes spurred us on, the odd, "that's not normal" has helped us to know that in this way our child is unique.

Outside of our relatives, we have a number of people who have helped weave a net of safety below us. We can ascend to great heights with the confidence that a fall won't end it all. We have friends from church, some of whom Kobi and I have known since we were in our late teens and early twenties. There are a handful of teachers who taught at my school who we can lean on for wise counsel. One incident that struck me, was an 'intervention' that my staff staged when they convinced me to allow Caleb to skip the 4th Grade. He'd taken 2nd Grade twice because the school he'd attended wanted to keep him with kids closer to him in age. When he started at my school, my staff tested him and found he was scoring across the board well beyond 4th Grade, never mind 3rd. Those teachers forbade me to hold him back unduly and we're grateful for them standing up to their 'boss' the way they did because they were interested in the wellbeing of a child. The gifted community and academia have been very supportive from Dr. Davis and Dr. Joy Harris, to a few members of MENSA. More recently, we've received overwhelming support from Chattahoochee Tech, Georgia Tech (especially the Aerospace Engineering faculty), the local news media (La'Tasha Givens!!!) and a number of non-profits (special shout out to Ms. Page and the rest of the Steve and Marjorie Harvey Foundation who gifted Caleb a scholarship for his undergraduate degree). We feel loved.

What are your son's favorite subjects in school and hobbies?
My son enjoys fencing and nearly earned a black belt in Tae Kwon Do. His other hobbies are Japanese spinning tops, called Beyblades. He also still likes collecting Transformers. His favorite subjects in school vary. He is starting to enjoy math, chemistry and physics, but he has always been drawn to literature and history. If he could learn for learning's sake, he would be a very happy person.

What are three of the greatest challenges of raising a Black male prodigy?
The three greatest challenges to raising a Black male prodigy in the United States are: crushing stereotypes and stigma, and keeping him alive for him to reach his potential. Addressing stereotypes and stigma is actually two challenges in one because on one hand there are persistent negative stereotypes to contend with and on the other hand, Caleb then becomes a 'unicorn.'

What advice do you have for parents of other highly gifted Black students?

○ Be intentional about exposing your child to new, hands-on opportunities to learn.

○ It is worth the investment, do not give up.

○ Find your network of support.

○ Teach your child character. They may be naturally intellectually gifted, but grit and character can only be learned.

○ If your child is still young enough for you to provide them with mostly educational toys, then do it.

What advice do you have for educators who may have a highly gifted Black male student in their school?

If you are an educator and you suspect you have a highly gifted Black male student in your class, the most important first step is to assume the best. Start with assuming that maybe this child is gifted and test him. What I mean is that, we all remember the 'Pygmalion Effect' study which highlights that children live up to the expectations we have for them. Many gifted males, particularly Black males who are gifted are not identified as such. The gifted school I started was full of boys who acted out in the schools they were in previously because they were bored, misunderstood, and intellectually malnourished. It may be challenging but educators are taught to scaffold lessons to use the same material to teach lessons at multiple levels. Withholding challenging material from a gifted child is a disservice to that child, his or her family, the community and all of us who may benefit from the uniqueness and talent they could bring to the world. Let's not live in regret or missed possibilities. It is far better for all of us to believe in a child's capabilities than to assume the worst.

Questions answered by Haley, 16-year-old law school student

What are your first memories of 'being different' as a gifted learner? How old were you? What were you engaged in?

My first memory was when I was in 2nd grade, around eight years old, and I asked more questions than the rest of my peers. Unlike everybody else, I did not hesitate to speak up when I was confused, nor did I hesitate to push the lesson further to gain more information. My second-grade teacher hated me for this, I think she felt I was challenging her when in actuality I was curious and wanted to learn more interesting, higher level material.

When you started school, can you recall your favorite games to play, things to do, hobbies, etc.

I have always loved math and music. I also enjoy gaming with my siblings. I write and perform spoken word poetry. I also love to read.

How did your family encourage you as a learner?

My story started with our local "good" suburban school district failing my siblings and me. My parents had requested multiple times that our school district test me for their Gifted and Talented program. Each time my parent's request was rejected. As additional issues popped up with my school and teachers, my parents decided to have me privately tested by an education psychologist. My testing came back as highly gifted and my parents received many recommendations on how to ensure I make a successful path in my education journey.

My parents became very deliberately active in helping shape my education. My mother took time to understand the education options that were available to our family. My mother decided to homeschool us. By doing this, she allowed her and my father to take full control of our education journey. My parents took our education seriously. In addition to planning our primary education homeschool activities, they ensured that our extracurricular activities were well-rounded. We did the normal activities of sports and music. We also had activities that supported us within our community to ensure that we had exposure to positive role models. But beyond that, my parents made the specific decision that we had academic extracurricular activities also. These were math, STEM, speech and debate, and more.

My parents made sure that we understood that academics and scholarly pursuits were important. Every opportunity was made to ensure that academics were reinforced. So when I decided to start early college my parents were very supportive. They helped me prepare for ACT and other tests. They allowed me to start college courses at my local community college. Their support ensured that I could take the path that I chose to take.

Additionally, my parents made sure that my siblings and I are encouraged to pursue our own academic excellence on our timeline. My parents never discouraged us and were supportive when we took efforts.

How did your family help you deal with challenges? Like being different, smarter than other students around you, non-acceptance by peers or even other family? Being a student of color in predominately white environments? Other challenges.
My family helped in so many ways, but a common theme is my mom. Say in second grade when I asked way too many questions; or in fifth grade when I started to become less outspoken, ask less questions, and cared less about learning; my mom served as a reminder for me that these people did not matter as much as I thought they did. She constantly explained to me that who I was should not be determined or influenced by others. When I knew all the material in middle school, my mother would advocate for me to move up to higher grades and take more complex material so I stayed engaged. When her advocacy was not changing the opinion of my public school, because of my race, she pulled me out and homeschooled me. My family, especially my mother, always approached our challenges as a family and my challenges as a student as an opportunity to learn and improve.

Can you think of any specific incident that you believe was pivotal in your acceptance of your giftedness?
One of the biggest moments is when I was pulled out of public school. The homeschool environment allowed me to learn at my own pace, stay engaged, explore my curiosities, and grow to my fullest. Because I was homeschooled, I was able to excel academically because I was in an environment tailored for me. This environment allowed me to fully express and fully grow into my giftedness, rather than tailoring myself and my abilities to what the teacher can tolerate or what my peers think is cool.

What are your academic and social interests?
My academic interests range from math to civil rights. I loved nearly all subjects after I started homeschooling and was able to really explore and appreciate all each subject had to offer. Social interests, to name

a few, are the piano, harp, reading, writing, coding, gaming, and building my own computer.

Are there other students like you in your current environment (age, gender, race, interests)? If so, can you share how having them in your environment helps or hinders. If not, would you like to have more people like you in your environment?
Yes, my siblings and friends I choose to surround myself with are like me. The beauty of homeschooling is your social experience is not chosen for you. Merely because you live near a similar building as 100 other students does not mean your best friend is one of those 100. Homeschooling allows you to expand your social circle to those of all ages, races, social economic classes, and locations without judgement or being outcast like a student would be at public school if they had no friends at school but rather had friends in another state.

What are your plans for the future?
Right now, I am in my second year of law school at SMU Dedman School of Law. My undergraduate degree is in education. It is my hope that I can use my undergraduate and legal education to continue to engage on education policy matters. I want to ensure that future generations of students are able to fully and equally access education opportunities. I believe that Generation Z will be the generation of Americans who take the next steps in the civil rights movement.

Is there anything else that you would like to tell parents raising highly gifted Black students?
My mother and I are always asked this question. We share that the most important thing a family can do is adopt a homeschool mindset. This mindset does not mean that a family has to homeschool. It means that you and your family prioritize education. That families commit to education for their children the same way that many do when chasing stage and stadium dreams. If we can invest in travel basketball and performing arts lessons, we can also focus on education opportunities that ensure a greater future for our community.

Update on Haley:

Haley Taylor Schlitz is 19 years-old and just graduated from SMU Dedman School of Law with her Juris Doctor. Haley is the youngest woman and youngest Black American to graduate from a law school in the history of the United States. In May of 2019, Haley graduated with honors with a Bachelor of Science degree from Texas Woman's University College of Professional Education and became the youngest graduate in the history of Texas Woman's University. On February 28, 2020, she was featured by Beyonce as one of Beyonce's This Is Black History 2020 honorees.

In April of 2021, Haley was named the host of the new online show Zooming In w/Gen Z that focuses on the experiences of Gen Z and highlights amazing young people in our nation. Haley served as one of seven national editors for the American Bar Association Law Student Division publications. Haley is also a recurring columnist for Blavity and Citizen Ed. She is pursuing a career as an attorney where she hopes to continue to advocate for education equity and greater access to gifted and talented programs for students of color and girls.

Questions answered by Khai's father (4 yr old male)

When did you first discover that there was something different about your highly gifted son?
When Khai was between six and eight months old I noticed that he would get extremely focused whenever a book or educational activity was presented to him. He would get so consumed in the pages and just study everything going on in the books. Early in his childhood I started him with educational cartoons. I didn't allow content that wasn't nurturing his mind. It got to the point that he himself would only want to watch educational cartoons or shows that were teaching him something. If we or someone played a normal cartoon without educational content, he would quickly lose interest, stand up and take off running to do something else. But if it was his favorite educational show or book, he would be so deep into it at times that I'd have to stop and check to make sure he was still awake. When he couldn't speak well

and read yet he would take long moments to look over everything before turning the pages. His attention span was extremely long for his age.

What was he like as a toddler? What kinds of toys did he play with? How about his sleep habits?
As a toddler, Khai oddly didn't care to play with toys with the exception of cars. It got to the point where we quit buying very many toys. Khai loved to watch educational cartoons.

When did he first learn to talk and begin to read?
Khai was making out words pretty good around 1 year old. He started reading entire books by age two. We recorded him reading his first full book at age two and shortly after, he had read every entry level book we could find him. By age three he had read over 50 or 60 books. As for sleeping habits, he would sleep through the night pretty well. Honestly, we didn't really set a bedtime as we should have. So there were many times he would be up pretty late for a toddler. Since he was an only child, he would sleep with me and his mom for much of his first couple of toddler years. It wasn't something we planned but it was tough to deny him.

Who are some of the people in your support system?
I grew up in foster homes. I spent half of my childhood in protective services. Now, as an adult and parent, my son and I are pretty much it. I'm blessed to have a fiancé who has welcomed my son into our little blended family. Khai does spend some time with his mom so I have some support from her as well.

What are your son's favorite things to do now, toys, school content, etc?
Right now, his favorite things are number blocks (his name for the snap blocks) he likes to organize them different ways and make things. He loves to play with toy fruits and vegetables. He loves preparing play meals. He also loves cars. As for educational materials, the list is endless, but I think his favorite right now is United States and Periodic Table games on his iPad. He also really likes to use the Duolingo app for his Spanish lessons.

What are three of the greatest challenges of raising a Black male prodigy?

Teaching him his true history. In my opinion, accurate Black history is fading out of the educational system. The architects of American history are making sure that our history starts at slavery. So just reinforcing my son's awareness despite what he is being exposed to in the school system is a challenge.

It's a challenge raising a Black male and watching out for the tactics that are being used to emasculate him. I'm believe everyone has a right to raise their child or children as they choose. I do not judge others, but I am very strict on what ideology is acceptable within my household. From the clothing, music and slang to religion, gender roles and sexuality. I am very strict.

Another great challenge is making sure that my son is an expert in financial literacy. I say expert because it is a thin line between those who are financially stable and those who are not. One can become the other in a day. But those who are wealthy are far from either. I challenge my son to be a scholar in the area of financial literacy so that he has the greatest chance at building wealth and passing it along to the next generation. I want to break the curse in my lifetime.

What advice do you have for parents of other highly gifted Black students?

Truly believe it in your mind and in your heart that your child or children are capable of being educated at the highest levels and reaching success in anything they touch. Once you believe it and have no doubts whatsoever, start implementing their education in everything they do, from replacing car ride music with educational songs and lessons to deleting distractions like TikTok and downloading educational games on their phones. Make education a lifestyle. And although it's never too late, start them early! And learn with your kids. I've learned so much myself by turning my house into an at home library and classroom. Buy them more books and less toys. Every Black family should have a bookshelf collecting books.

What advice do you have for educators who may have a highly gifted Black male student in their classroom/school?

I believe all children have a gift that hasn't been unlocked or discovered but if you do notice a child is displaying a talent for their education, challenge them. Our culture's future depends on educators identifying these children and pushing them to master their gift. That child may be the next president or scientist. I'd also like to see more educators pushing our children to learn financial literacy, politics, and artificial technology. We need our children building wealth, taking on more roles in policy making and being the frontiers of AI

Please also share any additional thoughts you'd like to with our readers.

I'd also like to see more Black parents and educators pushing our children to learn about financial literacy, politics, and artificial intelligence (AI) technology. We need more of our children learning about money and focused on building wealth at a young age. We need more of our children understanding government at an early age and taking on more roles in policymaking so we can start changing the narratives. And as crazy or complex it may sound we need our children competent in and learning AI. AI is inevitable and we need those who look like us being a large part of that industry.

CHAPTER 2

Unique Challenges of Being Bright, Talented & Black

*The struggles along the way are only meant
to shape you for your purpose.*

—Chadwick Boseman,
award winning actor, 1977-2020

Being gifted can be as much a challenge to gifted children as it can be to their parents. Many characteristics of giftedness raise concerns that need specialized attention from parents and school personnel. Without understanding the full scope of gifted behaviors, often even the most loving and caring parent cannot help a child tackle the external and internal challenges of being gifted. While many issues addressed in this chapter are those faced by all gifted children, Black gifted children face additional, specific dilemmas.

Anti-Black Racism and Its Impact on Gifted Learners

Black gifted children are more likely than any other demographic group to be under-identified and thus, underserved in gifted programs across the nation (Grissom, 2016). Black gifted children are likely to be treated unfairly, not only because of their ethnicity, but also because they are gifted, which creates additional challenges for them. Social justice advocates characterize the insults and discriminatory words, actions as "microaggressions" (Sue, 2020). Sometimes these microaggressions are overt and intended; other times these behaviors are more subtle, but harmful nonetheless.

Black gifted children are more likely than any other group to be discriminated against in school. Recent studies have made it clear that Black students with high achievement scores (the same as their white peers) are six times less likely to be referred for gifted education service. Black teachers are also more likely to refer Black gifted students for gifted programs. (Nicholson-Crotty, et. al., 2016). This poses a problem for many of our students, whose classroom teachers are more likely to be White than Black. Our nation still suffers from a lack of teachers of color in our schools.

Black students are also more likely to be subject to unfair discipline practices, especially in the southern states. We are also aware that Black girls are victimized by school practices and teacher behaviors. Black girls are unfairly treated as "more mature" and victimized by school disciplinary officers. For example, because Black girls may be more inclined to speak up and respond openly to adults, or in some cases, be physically more mature and independent, educators (especially by middle school) often typify them as being 'more mature'. (Cotton, Davis, Collins, 2022). Anderson (2020) advocates for improved teacher training and treatment of Black girls so that their gifts are recognized, and they have access to advanced programming suited to meet their high intellectual capacity. If your gifted child sees that she is not being treated or responded to by teachers in the same way as others, she will feel it on a deep level. The impact of this unfair treatment can be very detrimental to a young person's self-esteem over time.

Black gifted children in unfair or discriminatory school set tings understand from a very early age that something is wrong with their school experience. They often have a feeling that they don't quite fit with what the teacher expects or what their classmates are doing. This situation not only puzzles them, but over time, it becomes frustrating and disappointing. Some stu dents will try to make themselves fit in, even if it means that they are not being true to themselves. Others may withdraw within themselves or even physically withdraw from gifted programs. Some become depressed or angry and rebellious and act out. The low retention of gifted Black students in honors and advanced classes speaks to their discomfort level and the need for schools to examine better approaches to ensuring that students' intellectual and social-emotional needs are appropriately met.

Many gifted teens, both minorities and those in the majority culture, have a very deep concern for human rights, equity, and social justice issues in the community and the world at large. It is not uncommon for gifted students to become activists and leaders at an early age, not because others vote them into office, but because they feel personally obligated to speak up and work to help make a difference.

It is essential for parents of Black gifted students to teach their children about racism (Davis & Goudelock, 2020), describe to them what it means to be Black in America, talk about our history in this country, and help them understand, through your speech as well as your actions, that although they will face obstacles and challenges because of their race, they have the ability to be successful. Unfortunately, there have been numerous reports of police brutality and other unjust treatment of Black citizens that have appeared in the news media over the past five years. Many of these incidents have led to protests, not only locally, but around the world. Emerging from these unjust conditions has been a historical movement that began with the voices of college students and local advocates for justice that has swelled into communities across the nation and around the world. The Black Lives Matter movement has taken on a life of itself and has stirred the emotional sensitivity of gifted youth. The youth who have supported this movement come from diverse backgrounds around the world. It is important for families to understand that our most gifted youth are very empathetic and are moved to express their views against unjust treatment of communities everywhere. Your child may also be inclined to engage with other youth to express their opinions through organizations, protests, and sharing their views through their coursework. As a parent, your role is to listen, guide and provide the best advice you can to support your empathetic and compassionate preteen or teen as they participate in changing world conditions for people across population groups.

Lack of Understanding of Black Culture

Another barrier for Black children is simply a lack of understanding about Black culture from the majority population. When our schools were integrated, some even by force in the 1950s and '60s, Black students were placed in classrooms outside of their home communities. As a result, many Black students faced teachers for the first time who did not look like them and did not understand their behaviors, language, culture, and traditions.

Some researchers suggest that this lack of understanding is a major factor in the continuing achievement gap between Black children and White children, and they point to the increasing numbers of teachers who have little or no knowledge of and respect for who these students truly are, but yet who teach Black children on a daily basis (Edmin, 2017). As a result, these teachers tend to categorize and discriminate against Black students. Powerful research results from a nationwide study indicate that:

> *White male students are more than twice as likely to be placed in gifted/talented programs as are Black male students, while the latter are more than twice as likely to be classified as mentally retarded as White male students, in spite of research demonstrating that the percentages of students from all groups are approximately the same at each intelligence level. The persistent over-classification of Black male students as mentally retarded reflects, at best, a lack of professional development in this area for teachers and other staff.* (Nicholson-Crotty, S., et. al., 2016).

Scenario #2: *While waiting for a flight in a small airport a few years ago, I began a conversation with another traveler who I discovered was from the local area. As we began talking, I shared my profession with her and she commented that she was a local physician of African descent. As* *a first generation African, she began discussing some of the challenges of being an immigrant. I told her that I was a teacher education professor and taught a course in cultural diversity. I also have a module on immigrants that I truly enjoyed teaching. She later expressed her disappointment with the educational system and what she found to be discriminatory behavior of some educators and students. She shared with me a situation that her oldest daughter encountered in a summer science program on a college campus in a nearby state. My new acquaintance was Nigerian, dark skinned with a short 'afro' hairstyle like I wear mine. She remarked that her daughters resembled her and wore their hair the same. On the first day of the summer program, her daughter had a very disappointing experience. She told her mother that she was in a science class, the first class of the day and that she was the only female and the only Black student in the class. She said her daughter was uncomfortable, not because of the content matter, because she loved and excelled at science, but because her classmates whispered about her and did not make any efforts to sit nearby and make her feel comfortable. What was most upsetting was that one boy came close to her and said, "Are you sure you belong here?" She told him yes, but she was still uncomfortable. At the end of the class, she did as her mother had guided her—she went to talk to the instructor to report the way the boys were whispering and the question one asked aloud that made her feel so uncomfortable. Thinking that the instructor would ease her discomfort, she shared that she felt bullied. In turn, she said the instructor looked at her and said, "Let me see if you DO belong here," and looked at his roster to confirm that her name was actually on the class list. This type of bullying behavior increases the discomfort that Black students have in gifted and advanced learner programs and the sense that they are in "the wrong place" and have no business in advanced classes that may be predominantly White. Their sense of belonging in gifted programs is destroyed when their classmates and instructors are not welcoming in their behavior and seem to disrespect them because they are different in race or gender. As parents/guardians, we have to prepare our students for the potential that this may happen to them and teach them how to respond. Additionally, as parents/guardians, we must speak up to administrators and program leaders to ensure that teachers have cultural competency training and that all students are more sensitive to their peers and more invitational in their behaviors. These situations can be mitigated when we teach our students how to self-advocate and when teachers are more sensitive and teach social justice in all school environments.*

Responding to Anti-Black Racism

According to the National Association of Independent Schools, most Black students deal with some type of racism during their school experience. However:

> *In response to their experiences of racism, students reported feeling angry and strengthened most often.…. Feeling strengthened as a response to racism may seem counterintuitive. However, students who have been proactively racially socialized by parents and other adults so that they have coping responses ready when they encounter racism may report being strengthened because they were able to deal with racism in a healthy way. Indeed…students reported "speaking out" or "proving them wrong" as the coping responses they used most often.….*
> (Arrington, Hall, & Stevenson, 2003)

During the summer of 2020, the United States went through a pivotal moment in race relations. This moment was precipitated by the murder of George Floyd in the city of Minneapolis, Minnesota. Floyd's murder at the hands of a police officer triggered waves of protests by people across cultural groups all around the world. A video of his murder went viral worldwide, showing a police officer holding Floyd down, with his knee on Floyd's neck, for an extended period. Police officers said they suspected Floyd had used a counterfeit $20 bill in a local store (*NYTimes*, May 31, 2020). This grievous act on the part of one police officer raised awareness worldwide to a rising "culture of violence" against Black citizens by police officers around the nation. The empathy shown by people in almost every nation helped Americans recognize now was the time to do more to change conditions and relationships across cultural/racial groups; change relationships between police officers and the Black community; change the way that Black and other children of color were being educated in our schools and in general; work harder to provide a more equitable, humane, fair society for all. In school districts across the nation, there was an upsurge of interest in culturally-responsive teaching, anti-racist and social justice understandings, and improved conditions for students from all racial/cultural and income groups. These changes had to begin with training and with new policies and practices. Floyd's death precipitated an exciting time in school communities everywhere.

Parents, be aware that although racism is an unavoidable fact for our Black children, it does not have to be a destructive force against them. Do your part as community activists to ensure that our children are safe in their schools, in communities, and that they build the skills they need to be successful. Teach your children to be strong and emotionally healthy, to dispel stereotypes and myths about the Black culture, and to prove others wrong by doing well. Your children can rise above the racism they encounter, and in doing so, they can help others see that racism has no place in an equitable and fair society.

When educators discriminate because of a lack of appropriate professional development, the affected students are handicapped in their ability to receive educational opportunities that are equivalent to those offered to their majority-culture classmates.

Underestimating Black students

One way that discrimination and a lack of understanding of their culture affects Black children is that others simply do not expect enough of them—it is discrimination through low expectations. As a parent, you should be aware that teacher expectations contribute significantly to the way teachers teach and the way students learn. As a matter of fact, some scholars have concluded that teacher expectations, and thus the learning environment, have the greatest impact on student achievement (Ferguson, 2007). Teachers have the ability to strongly influence the lives of their students though the ways they interact with them and the amount of attention they give to them (or not) in the classroom.

Black students are faced with teachers in almost all situations who underestimate them and too often do not have the same expectations of Black students as others. Even in gifted and advanced program settings, Black students are underestimated and treated as if they are less intelligent than others (Copur-Gencturk, et .al. 2019). Teacher expectations are not unlike community and societal expectations. As a parent, you need to be alert to low expectations from various adults both within and outside of the school setting. Neighbors, relatives, coworkers, and potential employers often fall into the trap of low expectations, too, and it can be quite a challenge to keep your child from accepting those low expectations—and underachieving as a result.

Most children are negatively affected by low expectations and teacher bias. Some, however, use these expectations as motivators. One high school student from a low-income environment said this when asked about barriers or facilitators to her achievement:

> *When people see my home and my surroundings, they expect me to be of low education or incapable of educational success, because let's face it, that's the unavoidable stereotype. My environment encourages me to be successful in school in order to prove the stereotypes wrong.* (Davis, 2007)

Just imagine the numbers of children in classrooms and neighborhoods across America for whom underestimations and low expectations are the norm. They live in places where they are not expected to rise above or do anything fruitful with their lives. Among these children are many who have exceptional talents. Be alert for situations in which your children may be confronted with individuals who don't believe in their potential. For example, if your son tells you about specific comments made by teachers or others that indicate low expectations of him, immediately remind him of his high potential and how, with hard work and persistence, he has the ability to be anything he wants to be.

Too Black to be Gifted

In communities across the nation, Black gifted students are underestimated and too often seen as lacking the skills and level of intelligence to be characterized as "gifted." These stereotypical perceptions are systemic in nature and have followed Black gifted students across multiple generations. The world of giftedness has been seen as a world where only White or Asian students belong and Black, Brown, or other "minority" groups, even poor students, don't belong. This misperception is real and dangerously harmful. I have documented stories from parents and students over the years that have described how these painful characterizations are used regularly to describe Black gifted students. One story that always resonates around this phenomenon is of a Black gifted student athlete from a rural community:

Scenario #3: *Black gifted students' difference in language, demeanor, interests, communal concerns, creativity, and high intellectual capacity are not embraced as defining their uniqueness; instead, they are bullied and criticized as "too Black to be gifted" or "not Black enough." Being too Black then becomes like an ominous BLACK letter B worn on the back. Those who wear the letter are punished because they live between two worlds, navigating multiple social identities and intersectionalities, as defined by Kimberlé Crenshaw (1991).*

Several years ago, I interviewed a mother who was herself a former student in a gifted program that I coordinated early in my career. Her equally gifted son, D, attended both a rural high school, where he was a star athlete, and a selective regional part-time high school. D's mother told a distressing story of how her son was bullied by his White and Asian peers who attended the selective high school with him for being "too Black to be gifted." During the second half of the day, when he returned to his home school for additional classes and football practice, his peers from his community and church also taunted him, saying he was "not Black enough." D used linguistic styles derived both from the Black community, of which he as a proud member, and from his White peers who attended the academically gifted program. D's two souls were tested constantly, and he navigated successfully, but not without distress. It was his strength of spirit and the support of his family that kept him from being "torn asunder."

Excerpt from: Davis, J.L. (2022). "Too Black to Be Gifted": Linguistic Challenges Faced by Black Gifted Secondary Students: Where Can I Be My Whole Self? In A.H.C. Hudley, C. Mallinson, M. Bucholz (Eds). Talking College: the Linguistic Experiences of Black students in Higher Education. Teachers College Press (reprinted with permission),

If your child describes events that demonstrate that he is repeatedly subjected to other students or even adults who bully or taunt him for being a "smart" kid, talking differently, or having different interests than most students, set up an appointment with his teacher for a face-to-face discussion. After this meeting, if your child continues to describe negative comments that he and other students experience in the classroom, then your next meeting should be with the principal. It is important for parents to speak up and not allow students to be abused in school settings by adults who don't believe in their potential.

I caution parents to heed my son's advice and not let the school, other students, or adults, "bully the giftedness out of our Black students." Suffering from low expectations can destroy the spirit of anyone over time, particularly a gifted child or teen who is already in a minority and feels he has to prove himself time and time again. One mother passionately shared her feelings on this matter, saying that she had "a sense of responsibility to exalt her own son to let him know that he is special and capable of doing well in school and in life."

Internal Challenges

Overexcitabilities and the Gifted

Gifted children are generally more intense, more sensitive, and often respond to emotional situations more deeply than others their age. It is important for you as a parent to know that when you witness your child displaying these types of behaviors, it is not an indication that something is wrong with her. She is simply behaving in a way that comes naturally to her. Gifted children tend to have more energy (particularly when involved in activities of great interest); are more curious; have heightened senses of sight, hearing, smell, taste, and touch; feel more deeply and express these feelings openly; and talk and think faster than they can write, which sometimes results in barely-legible writing.

These types of intense behaviors were defined many years ago by Polish psychiatrist and psychologist Kazimierz Dabrowski, who worked with gifted adolescents and adults. Dabrowski called the intense behaviors of gifted individuals "overexcitabilities." According to Dabrowski, there are five categories of overexcitabilities. Examine Table 2 to see if any of the categories pertain to your child.

Table 2. Overexcitabilities of Gifted Children and Adolescents

Overexcitability	Description of intense behaviors (with negative manifestations of sensitivities to be aware of)
Intellectual	Thirst for knowledge, discovery, questioning; love of ideas/theories; constant searching for truth; detailed visual recall; detailed planning; keen observation; thinking about thinking; introspection *(sometimes very critical; argumentative)*
Emotional	Great depth and intensity of emotional life expressed in wide range of feelings, from great happiness to profound sadness or despair; strong emotional attachments; compassion; sense of responsibility; constant self-examination; responding at an adult level to spiritual experiences *(timidity; shyness; difficulty adjusting to new environments; depressive moods; feelings of guilt)*
Psychomotor	Restless; constantly moving; fast talking; intense drive; augmented capacity for being active and energetic; compulsive talking/chattering *(nervous habits, such as tics, nail-biting, and hair pulling)*

Sensual	Enhanced refinement of the senses: sight, hearing, smell, taste, touch; delight in beautiful objects, sounds of words, music, nature; intense dislike of certain textures, visual images, smells *(easily distracted by sounds or the feel of clothing seams or tags; may be inclined to overindulging behaviors, such as overeating or shopping sprees)*
Imaginational	Vivid imagination; frequent use of image and metaphor; richness of association; frequent and vivid dreaming; imaginary friends; inventions; gives toys and other objects personalities; preference for the unusual and unique; creation of private worlds; low tolerance for boredom; need for novelty and variety; love of poetry, music, and drama *(mixing truth and fiction; preference for imaginary over real friends)*

Overexcitabilities are assumed to be innate—a genetic predisposition of the nervous system to respond more intensely to life's stimuli. This causes those with strong overexcitabilities to have more intense experiences than are typical for individuals who do not experience overexcitability. As a result, some people may reject overexcitable children (and adults, too) for being "too intense," "too emotional," or "too sensitive."

Being aware of your children's overexcitabilities will help you understand them better and allow you to assist their teachers and other family members in being more sensitive to them (Piechowski, 2006). With appropriate guidance, children's overexcitabilities can become a real strength and source of high achievement; without such support and direction, their overexcitabilities can create problems. Often, gifted children show a lack of patience and tolerance with people who are not as sensitive as they are. Teaching your children respect for others who are different from them is important. Helping them accept and deal with their overexcitabilities is also important.

Intellectual overexcitability manifests itself in a seemingly unquenchable desire to know and understand. This can be seen in children who want to know everything about all sorts of topics, or it can present itself as a deep and insatiable thirst to learn everything there is to know about a particular topic of interest. These children are often quite independent, learning and investigating on their own, so it's important to direct them to credible sources of information and not to simply answer their questions. These children are typically very excited to go to school, but their knowledge often far surpasses their age peers, and their judgment lags behind their intellect. Consequently, they may find themselves without friends, as classmates become bored with their excited discussions on topics of little interest or understanding to them. They may also become disillusioned with teachers who seem to be going so slowly and who don't want them blurting out answers in class to questions that other children don't yet know. It will be critical for you to reassure your child that there is nothing wrong with wanting to learn, but you must also teach him that not everyone is excited about the things that excite him. In addition, he may need to learn that others don't necessarily like to be corrected all the time, and other students need a chance to answer the teacher's questions. Most importantly, however, you need to find intellectual peers for your child so that his animated thinking and speech can be shared with kindred spirits. Even one such child can become a lifelong friend if their interests are aligned.

Emotional overexcitability can be seen in children who are deeply sensitive to their own feelings and the feelings of those around them. These children seem to overreact to situations that might cause only mild reactions in others. For example, an emotionally excitable child may cry uncontrollably over the loss of a pet for days, or she may weep bitterly after seeing a movie with a sad ending. Parents need to remember that these emotions are very real to the child experiencing them, and they must handle the situation accordingly. Such a child will require very sensitively handled conversations about her concerns—discussions that validate her emotions, but can perhaps help her to put things in proper perspective.

A physically overexcitable, high-energy child (*psychomotor overex-citability*) may exhaust those around him as he exerts his virtually unending supply of energy. This child moves all the time, even while he's sitting still. He can't help but to tap his feet, jiggle his pencil—he even talks quickly. Adults need to give this child plenty of opportunities to move around, perhaps even while reading or studying. Projects that enable him to use his hands as well as his mind will help, but in his zeal, he may need to learn how to manage and organize his time to accomplish tasks. Parents and teachers need to be careful that such a child is not incorrectly labeled as hyperactive or as having ADHD.

A child who is *sensually overexcitable* will very often complain about the tags in the back of his shirts bothering him or the seams in her socks annoying her. The hum of fluorescent lights overhead or other such noises can disturb and distract these children enough to keep them from concentrating on classwork. Parents may need to run a fan or use another type of "white noise" machine in their rooms at night so that the children can sleep. In some cases, certain tastes or smells may make these children physically sick, or they may be quite sensitive to touch. While it is possible to help some children deal with irritations that they will encounter on a daily basis, the reality is that parents simply have to be patient with these children and try to help eliminate the things in their environment that bother and distract them. Over time, with interventions from parents and teachers, most children learn to be less sensitive in this area or at least learn ways to manage it.

Some children have *imaginational overexcitability*. These children like to fantasize, and they can be quite creative and dramatic when they write or tell imaginative stories. Some of these children construct very elaborate personas in their heads. As a parent, you may be well aware of your young child's imaginary friends, and you may even worry about the depth of her make-believe world. However, as long as your child can give and receive affection and can play with others, you can relax. Imaginary playmates are generally a sign of creativity and almost always disappear when the child goes to school or when a younger sibling is born. Acknowledging your child's invisible friends will encourage her creativity and convey to her that you respect both her and her inventiveness.

Acceptance is the key to raising healthy children when it comes to all the overexcitabilities. When I review Table 2, I see behaviors that were expressed by all my children as they grew up, and now, I see the same types of overexcitabilities in my grandchildren. I think that part of my job was helping my children learn to use their intensities and encouraging others to accept them. Having overexcitabilities is the norm for gifted children. Teaching your children to accept their natural inclinations and still function in a world that often does not understand them is important.

Idealism and Empathy

Their intellectual, imaginational, and emotional overexcitability often leads gifted children toward idealism. Because of their intense sensitivities to the world around them, gifted children and adolescents are often very idealistic—they can envision the possibilities of how things should be. They sense that "all is not well with the world," and they feel disappointment and frustration. Why do some people treat others in the mean, disrespectful ways that they do? Why do we have so many homeless people in such a wealthy society? Why do adults do and say things that they really don't mean, sometimes even lying and cheating?

These feelings may be apparent in gifted children's conversations, during which they reveal the seriousness of their concerns about the needs of others or the depth of their grief over events such as environmental disasters. They have a keen awareness of how the world—and sometimes they or their families—are falling short of what could be, and many of them want to try to do something to correct the injustices.

What a wonderful opportunity this is for parents and teachers! If the world is ever going to become a better place, it will be because of people who think and dream about how it might be—and then do something to change it. Think about the men and women who have changed the world in areas such as civil rights, women's rights, environmental causes, and political issues. It is vital to nurture this idealism in our children, as well as the resilience and perseverance that are also needed with it. If adults around them do not understand the depth of their disappointment and frustration, children's idealism can easily turn into depression, cynicism, and anger. In fact, it is likely that many of our rebellious and troubled youth are really very bright, intense, and creative, but also extremely disappointed in the hypocrisy and shallowness that they see around them.

How can you nurture idealism in your gifted child? First, look at what you are modeling in your family. Do you talk about family and social values? Do you also model these values though your behaviors? Too many parents drift into a pattern of "Do as I say, not as I do," and their children notice the behaviors far more than the words. It helps, too, if you can make sure that your children are involved in groups that are idealistic and that support your values. It is hard to remain an idealist when you are alone; it is easier if you are with others of like mind. Reading about others who survived discrimination, hypocrisy, and deceit can also help your children maintain their upward striving and personal and moral development.

Underachievement in Gifted Children

All of these factors—discrimination, lack of understanding, low expectations, and failure to understand a child's overexcitabilities or idealism—can result in the underachievement of gifted children. Just because your child is gifted, there is no guarantee that all of his grades will be A's and B's. As a matter of fact, gifted children rank high among underachieving students nationwide. Although underachievement strikes boys more often than girls, girls are not immune, and it is a serious dilemma for schools, teachers, and parents. However, there are strategies you can use that will increase your child's chances of conquering underachievement challenges.

Underachievement is a discrepancy or difference between what a child is able to do and how she actually performs in school or the types of grades that she earns on school assignment. For example, suppose your daughter, who has been identified as gifted and who received excellent grades in elementary school, is now in middle school and suddenly begins to bring home C's, or even D's or F's. Or your son was doing very well in kindergarten, first, second, and even third grade, but now, in fourth grade, he has begun to lose interest in school, puts little effort into his homework, or is scoring low on classroom tests. What should you do?

First, make sure your child knows that you are concerned. Your initial course of action should be to sit down and talk with him. Find out how his classes are going, what types of activities take place in the classroom, how well he gets along with his classmates, and what type of relationship he has with the teacher. Find out what your child is learning in school. Make this a habit by having an informal conversation each day. A few questions you might ask are:

- Did you learn something new in school today?

- What did you learn that was exciting or different from other ideas you have learned in school?

- Is there anything else that is happening that you were excited about. How about anything that bothered or disturbed you?

- Were your materials interesting or were they materials that you have used before?

- What kinds of books did you read today? Did you do any writing? How about science experiments?

Try to get an understanding of the attitudes toward achievement—by your child or school. There are many reasons why gifted children underachieve, so it may take a while to figure it out. Remember, gifted children were not born underachieving, so something is going on that is preventing them from living up to their potential.

Of course, you want to make sure that there isn't some physical problem that is interfering with your child's ability to learn and function in school. Sometimes children need glasses or have problems hearing, but parents and teachers may not notice this until third or fourth grade or even later. Also, being an intense child takes a lot of energy, and gifted children are more likely to need mid- morning and mid-afternoon snacks that are high in protein (like meat or cheese sticks) to replenish their reserves; otherwise, they may have trouble concentrating and become overly emotional.

Most often, though, underachievement is related to social or emotional issues that present themselves in the classroom or at home, and it can be specific to a particular class or subject area. Students who underachieve in one area may be quite successful in another that is of greater interest to them. As one expert on the topic of underachievement said, gifted children are seldom unmotivated; they just aren't motivated where we want them to be. Your son or daughter may be extremely interested in playing computer games or practicing dance moves but may lack the motivation to learn grammar or spelling rules.

Black gifted children are also subject to be teased or taunted in school just for being different. As parents you must always listen for any cues and watch for any changes in behaviors, or changes in peer groups. Unfortunately, some children are not empathetic and can treat others in a cruel manner. If you notice something different, it is important to have a conversation with your child and always maintain a relationship with your child that will allow him to feel comfortable telling you "anything." You are your child's first and best advocate. In order to advocate effectively, you must understand and be sensitive to your gifted child's needs.

Maintaining motivation to learn in school is a major challenge for gifted children, their teachers, and their parents. Numerous studies show that gifted learners report boredom in classroom instruction because of lack of challenge, limited opportunities to choose assignments, and classroom content that seems irrelevant and uninteresting to them. This can be a particular problem if the teacher already has low expectations for the Black students in the class. Keeping gifted students stimulated is especially difficult when teachers are not appropriately trained in gifted education curriculum and instructional strategies, as well as when access to complex and unique materials and activities are limited.

Another reason why achievement suffers in some gifted students is because of peer pressure. Being "too smart" can make these stu dents stand out from their peers, and if gifted learners have a strong desire to fit in with their classmates, they may purposely underachieve to be like them. If your gifted child is "dumbing down" to fit in with friends, you can explain to her that true friends will accept her for who she really is, and her path to success will not necessarily be the same path that everyone else takes. Be cautious that your child is not having experiences that feel as if he is "having his giftedness bullied out of him." That phrase was shared with me by my son as we had a conversation about his own gifted son and challenges in school that may match with experiences that he had as a youngster being bullied by other students who teased and taunted him for being "smart," "being gifted," and even for "talking differently" than other students,. Teach her the value of being true to herself and her standards and principles, that accomplishing work that she can be proud of is a worthwhile endeavor, and that fitting in with others may seem critical now but will likely seem much less important as she matures.

Underachievement can also occur if a gifted child is in a power struggle with a teacher or with parents. Sometimes it is simply that the child is not willing to participate in what, to him, seems silly— for instance, "I'm not going to show you how I got the answer! I did it in my head because it's so simple." A more serious situation occurs when the child underachieves as a way of getting back at his parents. "You can make me go to school or stay in my room, but you can't make me get good grades!" This kind of parent-child relationship is badly damaged and needs repair, and while school performance is important, you must remember that your relationship with your child is more important than the grades he gets. Also remember that severe punishment and yelling are not likely to increase your child's grades or help your rela- tionship. There are other things you can do, as we will discuss later, but try to extract yourself from no-win power struggles. If your child's anger, rebellion, or power struggle is close to reaching these levels, parents should seek the help of a professional—a psychologist, coun- selor, or minister—preferably one who knows something about gifted and talented children and adolescents and who can coach parents about these issues. Where serious under achievement is occurring or seems likely, parents and students may also benefit from reading the books *Being Smart about Gifted Learning* by Mathews & Foster and *Gifted Teens Survival Guide* by Delisle & Galbraith.

Not only is academic achievement influenced by external factors, such as slow-paced classrooms, peer pressure, and power struggles, it is also affected by students' internal motivation. High internal motivation can help children withstand many outside pressures to underachieve. This internal motivation is often referred to as an "internal locus of control." We can help our students develop it by making sure that they are placed in supportive classroom environments where achievement is celebrated and where their self-esteem is continuously nurtured. These children learn to put forth effort to accomplish their tasks because they want to succeed and attain the satisfaction of a job well done. Students without an internal locus of control will only perform tasks because they are told to do so; these students are motivated by an "external locus of control," such as grades or praise, and they are more likely to be influenced by peer culture. Externally motivated students' drive to achieve comes from others, rather than from standards or guidelines that they have set for themselves.

Students who are externally motivated more often experience underachievement than do students who are internally motivated. However, when gifted students are enrolled in culturally supportive school programs that set high expectations for them, their internal motivation to achieve is strengthened, and the tendency to underachieve is lessened. Another way to encourage motivation is to group gifted students for at least part of every day with others who learn and think as they do—with academic peers. When a gifted student is "the only one," it is easy to slack off because the work is so easy. If these students are placed with other gifted students, they can all be given assignments that are rigorous and challenging, which will stimulate them intellectually while also allowing them to bounce ideas off one another in group discussions. Gifted students enjoy being with others who think as they do. Placing them in an environment of "like minds" can make their learning experiences much more pleasurable—which in turn increases their motivation to achieve.

What else can you do to help your children develop an internal locus of control? Here are a few ideas:

○ Create learning opportunities at home that focus on areas of their interest. When children feel that their interests are valued by the adults around them, they are more apt to believe in themselves and their abilities.

○ Be a model of learning. Let your children see you reading, learning to solve problems, and becoming better at things you aren't yet really good at.

○ Give them choices, including the choice to fail, by setting the fewest limits that you have to—and at an early age, rather than when they get older. Children who learn to manage themselves early in life tend to have a better internal locus of control. These choices may be what to wear, what books to read, what friends to play with, etc. Of course, this freedom needs to be within limits; you can't let a child have unlimited choices. You are in charge of the family. Maintaining that control is critical as your child develops and continues to look to you for your wise counsel. However, avoid power struggles. Setting firm limits means that you are less likely to get sucked into squabbles, and allowing children freedom within those limits lets them experience the natural consequences of their choices. So pick your battles, try to set only those limits that you really can enforce, and then be consistent about enforcing them.

○ Expose your child to professionals and experts across a variety of fields. When children are around adults who value education, working in areas of interest, and achievement, they are more likely to value it, too. They want to be like these adults.

○ Have your children maintain a diary or journal of daily activities, and make sure that they include school assignments and special projects in it. This helps them organize themselves, and it also allows them to keep things in perspective. When you look back at the terrible worry that you wrote about in your diary several days ago, it now looks almost silly. How could you have been so worried?

○ Maintain regular contact with your children's teachers in elementary, middle, and high school. Often, parents are very involved with schools when their children are young but become less so as their children enter middle or high school. Your children growing older is no reason for you to back off, even if they ask you to. You still need to monitor school attitudes, achievement, and progress. However, be careful not to "hover" around school and be a pest to teachers. You can carefully and considerately show you care without being at school each day or being insensitive to the fact that the teacher is also responsible for other students and other duties.

○ When your children express frustration with school tasks or assignments that may be new or different, try to find out what the teacher really expects. Of course, sometimes kids exaggerate and try to get sympathy from parents, so you may need to be in touch with the teacher directly.

○ Listen to your children share their concerns about school, even if those concerns seem trivial to you. Consistent conversations, with a lot of listening, help to establish trusting relationships between parents and children. Lecturing or talking at a child seldom does much good.

○ When you talk with your children, ask if the school material is understandable, challenging, or even too easy. Sometimes a student can negotiate a "Learning Contract" with the teacher that will allow her to work ahead or on alternative projects once she has shown reasonable mastery of the regular classroom work. Ask if there are special projects for which she needs extra materials, and remind her to always come to you for support.

○ If extra materials pose a financial burden, talk with the teacher about other options. The teacher should be willing to provide alternatives that do not place an undue burden on any family.

In a recent book on self-advocacy, expert authors share how to work with students from underrepresented gifted populations to speak up and ask for what they need from their education (Davis & Douglas, 2021). As they self-advocate, students can articulate the kind of instruction, independent studies, or even extracurricular activities that are most fulfilling, based on their interests, strengths, and plans for their future.

As a parent, you want to make sure that your child knows how important it is to you for him to realize his dreams. However, parents must find a balance between high learning expectations and pressure to succeed. Pressuring a student to achieve for the sake of making good grades can backfire. Underachievement is tied closely to self-concept, and children who feel that their best efforts aren't good enough eventually begin to place self-imposed limits on what is possible. If their parents (and teachers, too) frown on every paper or project that isn't perfect, these children may think, "I'm just not a good student." Likewise, if your child brings home a report card with seven A's and one B, try to avoid pointing to the B and saying, "And what happened here?" You can talk about the B, but first talk about what the child did right.

I am not suggesting that you lower your expectations. It is important that you encourage your child to do her best. However, being gifted does not mean that your child will always get good grades or behave in an appropriate manner. Gifted children need gentle guidance and support from the important adults in their lives, and their parents are the most important of these adults.

Boys

Black boys, in particular, underachieve in schools at alarming rates. Black males are suspended, expelled, and placed in remedial special education classrooms far more often than their White age peers. More than 20 years ago, Jewell Taylor Gibbs, Ph.D., a Black sociologist, revealed alarming statistics on these problems, as well as the impact that these conditions have on the educational, social, and psychological state of Black male students. She even labeled our boys "an endangered species." Health statistics and rates of incarceration, low school achievement, murder, and suicide all place Black males in a category by themselves. Since Gibbs' important research, numerous scholars and practitioners have worked to improve the schooling and life circumstances of Black boys, but problems persist.

Most of the time, when we discuss underachievement in Black male students, we look at students who are underperforming in school, and we focus on remediation and other alternatives for fixing the problem. However, it is equally important to identify and focus attention on high-performing Black male students, particularly those from impoverished areas. They may be doing average or even above-average work in their classes yet still be achieving far below their potential!

New research, books, and programs are now giving special attention to high potential and resilience in Black males. See the list in Appendix D for suggested reading. These studies and programs reveal what it is that enables gifted Black students to rise above challenging life circumstances, as well as how certain school experiences can either enrich their lives or serve as another form of societal oppression. In general, boys who excel in school describe their families as more closely knit and supportive than those of boys who underachieve (Olenchak, 2002)

As an example, the authors of *Beating the Odds: Raising Academically Successful African American Males* describe the lives of college students who participated in a special program for high-performing students at the University of Maryland (Hrabowski, Maton & Greif, 1998). These young men came from challenging backgrounds, and yet they were very academically successful. Even with the odds against them, they excelled—according to the authors, in large part because their parents were described as maintaining regular contact with schools, having high expectations of their sons, and constantly praising and encouraging their boys.

Many successful enrichment programs share similar features:

- ○ Mentoring by successful Black males from similar neighborhoods or with similar backgrounds

- ○ Summer and after-school scholar programs with attention to positive racial identity development

- ○ Family support programs to involve families and teach them about the challenges faced by Black males as a minority in this culture

- ○ Grouping students in similar cultural groups and with those of the same gender so that they can participate in programs together

Even though programs such as these can supplement your child's learning and be a wonderful place for him to experience opportunities for success, as well as find friends with similar interests and abilities, it is important for you to recognize that your son's daily schooling experience may or may not be a nurturing environment. Rather than being havens of hope, schools—even those with special programs—can be places where Black boys are marginalized and stigmatized. Negative classroom interactions, comments from teachers, visual images, and informal and formal discussions, as well as a lack of respectful Black male role models in schools, all send a negative signal to Black boys, making school a place that students would rather "run from" than "run to."

Providing Black males with strong family, peer, and community relationships that focus on academic excellence is critical. During the tween and teen years, we often begin to lose touch with our boys. Access to males who support and demonstrate strong values and can provide future direction for boys will help to counteract strong, negative peer pressure, as well as other outside pressures to conform to low expectations. Fraternal organizations, community groups, value-focused family meetings, and summer and Saturday morning programs are all examples of the types of activities that can help maintain positive values in gifted and talented students.

One exemplary example of a program model focused on the achievement of Black male students is The Scholar Identity Model developed by Gilman Whiting, Ph.D. of Vanderbilt University.

Girls

Recent research on Black females indicates that Black girls as just as likely to be discouraged and underestimated as boys in public school settings (Anderson, 2020; Cotton, Davis & Collins, 2022; Morris, 2016) As a result, gifted Black females are among a high risk group in our schools. Teachers with minimal cultural competency training and sensitivity for the challenges faced by Black females may exist in any school environment. Families should be cautious and keep an open mind and ear when your gifted female who should be a high achiever begins to underachieve and her attitude towards school changes. It may be difficult to "see" underachievement occur in the beginning stages. It may show up as a change in attitude towards school and academic activities or a change in peer group, or your once lively, outspoken daughter may become quiet and hold her experiences privately so that no one knows how she is feeling or what may have occurred to precipitate the change in behavior. In math and science courses, girls often show lower performance than boys. This can stem from students being stereotyped by teachers, guidance counselors, and others who sometimes suggest to female students that they will have difficulty in these subjects or will not be successful in advanced, high-level coursework. Thus, many gifted Black girls are actually counseled away from taking high level coursework and then girls may eventually convince themselves that they can't compete with boys in these areas.

Challenging Gifted Girls

Sometimes children underachieve because they aren't challenged enough in class, and their motivation to do well is sapped by apathy. Some of these exceptionally bright children simply need to be intellectually stimulated by a rigorous curriculum, along with the company of a group of students as eager to learn as they are.

The Program for the Exceptionally Gifted (PEG) at Mary Baldwin University in Virginia is a unique, all-female program that allows bright girls as young as 13 years-16 years old to enter a residential college program, skipping up to four years of high school and graduating in four years with a bachelor's degree.

Exposing gifted females to historical accounts of women who have made contributions to (and were the first to excel in) traditionally male fields will also provide them with encouragement and motivation to achieve in school and set goals for the future. Recently, there has been a surge in interest in programming for high-potential and gifted Black females, particularly in the areas of Science, Technology Engineering and Math (STEM). An example is the technology focused organization "Black Girls Code." Black Girls Code provides instruction and support (for ages 7-17) from technology professionals of color in the areas of artificial intelligence, web design, robotics and related areas. Their goal is to "build pathways for young women of color to embrace the current tech marketplace as builders and creators." For more information about their services, visit their website at www. blackgirlscode.com.

Another problem that gifted girls often experience that can lead to underachievement is perfectionism. Some girls believe that they must perform perfectly, and if they cannot do something perfectly, they suffer extremely high anxiety. They may spend days on projects or even refuse to complete or turn in assignments that don't meet their impossibly high standards, thereby driving down their grades. Sylvia Rimm, Ph.D., an expert on underachievement, notes that many gifted children "are so highly competitive that they don't dare take the risk of making an effort for fear they will fail to meet their own too-high expectations." Parents of children who suffer from the paralyzing fear of not being perfect need to teach their children that attaining true perfection is impossible, and sometimes "good enough" is indeed good enough. Being human means that you are less than perfect. Perfectionism as a trait of giftedness has been studied and documented by psycho-social researchers for years. Research studies have provided descriptions of how perfectionism affects students and strategies for parents and educators to use to mediate the negative effects of perfectionism.

Perfectionism so extreme that it becomes debilitating can be found in gifted boys, but it is more commonly a problem experienced by girls. Girls also tend to place a great deal of importance on their physical appearance and their social acceptance within their peer groups— more so than boys, although boys sometimes run into problems in this area as well. However, the desire to look like and be liked by their classmates most often affects female students. When they don't fit in because of how they look (or for any other reason, which might include aspects of their giftedness), girls can experience unhappiness, isolation, and possibly even teasing or bullying—all of which can lead to underachievement.

On the bright side, gifted girls who are different from their peers sometimes focus more on academics than on social issues in school. When they don't have many peers or opportunities for social interaction, they can focus their energies on areas of their lives that are more satisfying for them, like doing well in school, as opposed to struggling with social interactions that leave them feeling inadequate. Trying to look like their peers can feel to them like a losing battle—one they don't want to bother fighting.

Depending on the environment, Black girls may have the additional burdens of skin color, hair, and class status to contend with. In a chapter written by students attending a school for the gifted in Florida, one of the students (a Black female) shared the challenges of being in an environment through most of her school career where she as the only Black female. Challenges included isolation, feeling different because of her skin color, and not having peers or teachers who understood some of her unique challenges, even the challenge of having hair that was different from others (Konuru, 2021). She shared how affirming it was when she was able to attend a summer camp on the campus of an Historically Black College (HBCU) where other females were like her, Black and gifted. This feeling encouraged her to join a student advocacy group working to help their school increase the numbers of students of color attending the school.

Gifted Black girls need to know that it is okay to look different from their classmates, and that achievement and success do not necessarily come wrapped in the same packages as everyone else. You can remind them, too, that the peer pressures to look and act like everyone else will be greatly reduced once they are beyond high school.

The Role of Guidance Counselors

Guidance counselors should be an ally to gifted children in all schools. A lack of training in gifted education and cultural competency limits the ability of guidance counselors to meet the needs of gifted students from minoritized populations. Additionally, guidance counselors are often so overwhelmed with other duties, such as coordinating school testing, that they have only minimal time to assist gifted students with special issues as they go through their high school programs. Even more problematic, some guidance counselors in racially integrated high schools actually have counseled Black gifted students out of advanced placement (AP) and honors courses—again, a barrier of low expectations.

Some Black parents have also experienced counselors discouraging their children from taking advanced coursework have responded by meeting with the counselors to demand that their sons and daughters be given the right to take any coursework they desire. More recently, several high schools have implemented open enrollment policies for their advanced placement courses, which has increased the number of Black students successfully taking AP courses.

As a parent of a Black gifted student, it is very important that you establish a good relationship with the school counselor and the high school gifted coordinator to ensure that your child is enrolled in the appropriate courses and that he has access to any supports available to assist him with achievement and success. Counselors must be culturally competent and sensitive to the unique needs of Black students.

Underachievement and Peer Relationships

Underachievement in children and adolescents is often directly related to peer pressure. Peer pressure is a significant issue for many middle school and high school students today. Gifted children, of course, need friends, and often these friends can help establish an atmosphere in which the children are achieving and trying to do their best. However, peers can also create an atmosphere that does not support academic achievement, or they can even create one that inhibits it. There is enormous pressure for our children to fit in with others who may be focused on certain brand names or types of clothes or shoes or who use "street talk" as a means of distinguishing themselves from others and establishing a special peer group identity.

Parents need to understand that their children's circle of friends may begin to shift by the time they reach high school. Researchers have documented how as children grow older, they begin to separate themselves not just by age, but by race. Even though your child may interact with a mixed group of children in elementary or middle school, by high school, race becomes a significant factor in peer relationships.

Note from the author: It was my son who brought these changing behaviors to my attention. From preschool through middle school, he was friends with a small group of White boys, one of whose mother was his babysitter for two years, so he had actually stayed in their home for seven to eight hours on some days. One day, when I asked him about the boys, my son said, "I don't hang around with them anymore; they just recently discovered that they were White".

This experience could have caused a blow to my son's self-esteem and ego, but it didn't do much harm because our family support circle is large and strong. Although we teach our children what it means to be Black and to have pride in family and in themselves, we continue to welcome people of all races into our family circle.

Later, one of my son's closest friends, once again a White boy, began picking up habits from my son and his other Black friends, and I'm sure he was accused from time to time of "acting Black"– ironically.

It is important for parents to help their teens learn to use good judgment when deciding who their peers are and who they want to identify with. Open and honest conversations about the benefits and consequences of the friends they choose to hang out with are always beneficial. You may need to talk about the people that you yourself choose to be with, and the ones you don't, so that your children can learn the difference between acquaintances and friends. Your children need to know that they can talk to you if they have problems and that they can be honest with you in sharing their feelings about serious matters like drug use, alcohol abuse, early sexual activity, fighting, bullying, and skipping school. These are all topics of conversation that children, tweens and teens engage in among themselves on a regular basis, but they are ones that parents too often avoid.

Many children, particularly when they become teens, do not want their parents to comment on their friends, so it may be difficult to have open, non-judgemental, honest conversations on the pros and cons of engaging in certain social behaviors. As a parent, though, you must work to combat the terrific pressures on your children to be like others who may be negative influences on them and engage in behaviors that are unhealthy for them. Set boundaries around your children's social activities, establish curfews, demand to know who they will be with, and make it clear that there are certain places that they are simply not allowed to go. Your children may complain that you are meddling, so it is important to discuss the reasons why you have made your decisions, which is always more effective than saying, "Because I said so." If your children persist, simply respond by saying that you are doing this because you are the parent and you love your children. Try to help them understand that everyone has to deal with peer pressure on some level—including adults—and that people have to decide whether they will become followers or leaders.

Being members of certain rebellious social groups can seem exciting and be tempting in middle and high school. However, most gifted teens will be sensible and choose to do what is best, regardless of what their age peers may do. Even so, as a parent, you should make sure that your child is involved in at least some groups (i.e., band, church, camp, etc.) in which their peers are high achievers and academically oriented.

If your child is going to different classes at a new school and has not yet made new friends or is having difficulty doing so, feelings of isolation can cause a sudden drop in grades and a lack of interest in school. The emotional impact of positive or negative social experiences in school can have a dramatic effect on academic performance. If your child must change schools, perhaps you can make an effort to find a social group in the neighborhood, church, or a community organization while your child is getting accustomed to the new school environment. This will ease the transition to the new school by providing your child with some social and intellectual peers who share some things in common.

Some children spend large amounts of time alone and may not seem to need peers or involvement in social groups as much as other children or teens. If your child is alone by choice because she enjoys the solitude of reading or playing music, for example, you should not force her to engage in social activities which she may dislike or which may make her uncomfortable. Understanding and appreciating her need for alone time will keep her from feeling that something is wrong with her. However, if your child seems lonely and spends time alone because she lacks the social skills that would enable her to join a peer group, you may need to intervene. She may need to learn social skills, or she may need help understanding what is reasonable to expect from peers. Search for one or two small groups in which she can feel safe, such as a church youth group or a Boys and Girls Club, where adult leaders help students develop social skills.

By the time they reach their teen years and begin to prepare for adulthood, your children are working toward developing their independence from you. The opinions and behaviors of their peers become powerfully influential, and you as a parent will have to work much harder to exert your influence over them. Sometimes you'll feel like your teens don't hear anything you say to them. At such times, you may want to remember what the writer Mark Twain said: "When I was a boy of 14, my father was so ignorant I could hardly stand to have the old man around. But when I got to be 21, I was astonished at how much the old man had learned in seven years."

Even though it may feel like an uphill battle at times, establishing open lines of communication when your children are young will certainly help you as they get older so that you can remind them in non-combative ways that their decisions now can affect them for the rest of their lives. Teaching your teens to think about long-term consequences is one of the best lessons you can give them.

Visual-Spatial Learners: Seeing the World in Pictures

Most teachers teach their students by lecturing them and assigning homework that involves the students reading material, taking notes, and demonstrating what they know through written assignments and tests. For many students, this method works just fine. However, some students simply don't learn this way. Their brains process information differently, and it is difficult for them to fully grasp information that is presented in this way. These children are called visual-spatial learners.

Visual-spatial students are much better at remembering pictures, scenes, or images, and thus, their visual memory is how they retain information. They learn by visualizing or by doing things with their hands. They have a good sense of where things are in space and how things fit together. Most of them possess a strong mechanical aptitude—they can look at a machine and know how it works. They don't talk things through, and they don't read manuals unless they have to. Reading or listening to words is simply not their preferred way of learning. As a result, these students are typically better in math, science, technology, and the arts than they are in reading and language arts.

A lack of exposure to books and reading in their developmental years can cause verbal limitations in some children. Some of them, particularly if they enter school without these kinds of early reading experiences, may be stronger as visual-spatial learners than as verbal learners. Unfortunately, having strong visual-spatial skills and weak verbal skills makes it difficult for visual-spatial learners to succeed in school. Many Black children have well-defined and recognizable visual-spatial strengths but are not identified as gifted because diagnosis usually relies on how well a person reads and interprets problems in language. Teachers—and parents, too—need to remember that there are various ways of learning, and all of them are important. In the case of visual-spatial learners, there are nonverbal tests available that can be used to identify giftedness. These tests are widely used today with Black, Hispanic, and other diverse groups that may have specific language deficits to measure their general ability.

Visual-spatial students often understand number systems and remember number problems more easily than their peers because they see these systems and problems in their mind's eye. They may also be exceptional at solving puzzles and playing certain board games, like chess. In fact, many inner-city educators and community leaders have found visual-spatial learners excel at playing chess, though their skills in reading may not be as strong. These same students will perform wonders when given a set of Legos or other construction building toys. They may also surprise adults when asked to manipulate the parts of a complicated machine by putting those parts together more efficiently and effectively than others.

In school, however, students are not often given opportunities to engage in the kinds of activities that demonstrate their visual-spatial abilities. (Anderson, 2014) Although individuals with visual-spatial gifts generally perform well in arts classes and geometry, technology, and preengineering courses, most school instruction, even in those classes, is often based on language. Teachers may see these students as deficient because they don't learn to read as quickly as others, nor do they enjoy reading as much as other children. In addition, they may find it hard to remember details unless they can visualize them. They can also be rather disorganized and do a great deal of talking, but not necessarily be able to put their thoughts down in writing. Fortunately, new information from brain research is helping educators to value visual-spatial learners and learn better how to work with them.

If you believe that your child is a visual-spatial learner because of the way he solves puzzles or is able to play complicated games like chess or Tetris, discuss his strengths with his teacher, and suggest that the teacher use instructional strategies and assignments that build on his strengths. Hands-on activities are especially helpful for these students. Your child's teacher should value and appreciate his visual-spatial giftedness. In addition to talking to your child's teacher, connect your child with professionals from different fields where visual-spatial skills are used, such as software developers, civil and mechanical engineers, architects, computer technicians, and graphic artists. If your child has exceptional visual-spatial skills and is interested in medicine, becoming a surgeon may be an option to consider.

At the middle school level, opportunities to participate in Odyssey of the Mind, Technology competitions, Lego Logo, science fairs, chess, and pre-engineering competitions can provide excellent outlets for your visual-spatial child. A good resource is the National Society of Black Engineers (NSBE), which sponsors programs (the Pre-College Initiative), offers scholarships, and provides a helpful website with links to many educational resources for students interested in math, tech ology, engineering, science, and other related areas. NSBE's website and phone contact information is located in Appendix B, along with other valuable resources for Black gifted children.

3e: Twice-Exceptional Gifted Children from Diverse Backgrounds

An area of concern for many years has been how to address the needs of a high-potential child who may also have a disabling condition. This could be a child who has a vision or hearing impairment, a learning disability, or some other physical or emotional challenge that needs to be considered. In gifted education, these students are referred to as "twice exceptional," and being twice exceptional and a member of a culturally diverse group—3e poses even more challenges for your child. In an article in the VARIATIONS publication, suggestions are provided for parents and educators (Davis & Cotton, 2021).

The National Education Association recently estimated that six million students across the country can be categorized as twice exceptional. The most common disabilities among gifted children are physical disabilities, learning disabilities (LD), and attention deficit disorders (ADD).

Raising a twice-exceptional child can pose particular challenges for parents. In school, the child's high ability can be overlooked or neglected because there is usually greater focus on the disability. In some instances, the child's gifts are masked by the disability; in others, the reverse happens, in which the child's gifts are such that the disability is unnoticeable, although the child only performs at an "average" level instead of at the high level of which she is capable. It can be very difficult for school personnel to identify these types of children for either gifted or special, remedial school services.

If you are a parent of a 3e child, you should certainly focus on addressing the child's disability so that he can grow and develop as "normally" as possible. However, addressing the child's high intelligence and high potential is equally important. Some of the challenges faced by twice-exceptional children include:

○ Inconsistent academic performance
○ Lack of organization and study skills
○ Difficulty with social interactions
○ Auditory or visual processing problems
○ Difficulty expressing ideas or "getting to the point"
○ High sensitivity to criticism

In schools, students with disabilities are protected by the federal government's Individuals with Disabilities Education Act (IDEA). IDEA requires that all students with disabilities be provided a free and appropriate education. Each student's educational and physical needs are evaluated using specific criteria, which are spelled out in a federal law known as Public Law 94-142. Within this law is a description of the role of parents in the evaluation process, as well as a requirement that students with disabilities have a written Individualized Education Plan (IEP) developed for them to ensure that their educational needs are met. If your gifted child has a defined disability, she will have an IEP. However, because gifted education is not federally mandated (required by law), gifted students' needs are only met according to state and local district requirements. Herein lies the challenge for parents of twice-exceptional children.

In serving twice-exceptional children, some schools are very progressive and have programming requirements in place to ensure that students receive instruction geared toward their intellectual level, in addition to support services for their disability. But just as gifted Black students are overlooked and lack access to gifted education programs, the same holds true for 3e students. As a culturally diverse twice exceptional student, your child is more likely to be underrepresented and not have access to programming that other 2e students may have. Some schools will only provide what is required by federal law and the IEP and may not accommodate your child's intellectual gifts and strengths. Gifted programming and other academic enrichment options present funding and staffing issues in each school district, and in some cases, especially when funds are limited, schools will provide only what is required.

This is where your advocacy as a parent comes in. Although your 3e child is guaranteed by law to receive services for his disability, you may have to insist that the school also provide for his giftedness. Hold frequent meetings with your child's teachers to discuss his progress, and be aware of any problems or concerns. Be sure that you also attend all parent-teacher conferences scheduled by the school, as well as Individualized Education Plan meetings so that you can provide your input as your child's educational plan is developed and implemented.

Most twice-exceptional children who are given the opportunities to develop their intellectual skills while their disabilities are being addressed go on to succeed at whatever they strive to accomplish.

Disabilities can be overcome when parents and educators work together to ensure that gifted students are offered academic options that will challenge them and allow them to stretch their minds. Being twice exceptional and Black is almost a triple challenge, as children must deal with being gifted, disabled, and a minority all at the same time. However, with the right support and encouragement, our children can accomplish greatness, despite the odds against them.

Meeting the Challenge

Black gifted children have many hurdles to overcome in our contemporary society. Because of racial discrimination, low expectations, and limited access to appropriately challenging curriculum and programs, they have to work harder than their majority-culture peers to prove themselves. They have to stand tougher than their average-ability classmates to triumph over the extra pressures and tribulations that can come from being gifted. However, the very things that create difficulties for our children are also the things that give them the power to succeed—their Black heritage and their giftedness. Let your children know that they have the potential to achieve their dreams. It may not be easy, but with your love and support, they will succeed.

CHAPTER 3

The Immeasurable Value of Family Involvement

Surround yourself with the dreamers, the doers,
the believers and thinkers; but most of all,
surround yourself with those
who see greatness within you,
even when you don't see it yourself.

—Simone Biles, One of the top gymnasts in
Olympic and world history

Living with a gifted child can be joyous as you experience firsthand his imagination, curiosity, quickness, ingenuity, and the sheer excitement with new ideas and understandings that set him apart from other children his age. You know that this child has the potential to contribute meaningfully in some way to society, his community, and his family. He may one day do something great! Your belief in this is grounded in a strong sense of hope for a better future for your child than you may have experienced for yourself.

Hope means trusting in what you cannot see but what you earnestly believe is possible. And with gifted children, the possibilities are innumerable. As a parent of a gifted learner, you may be struggling with issues related to your child's unique abilities. However, no matter what the circumstances of life are right now, your child has the potential to be a great person and to reach goals in her lifetime that others may not be able to accomplish.

In his second autobiographical book, President Barack Obama calls this "the audacity of hope."(Obama, 2006). Obama writes of his family's life circumstances, which were difficult at times, but his courage and optimism gave him hope. People in similar circumstances often have this same type of "audacity"—a boldness to believe in the potential for success, even in the midst of challenging situations. This is what we must do for our gifted children.

As the parent of Black gifted learner, you will face many challenges trying to provide what your child needs as she grows, learns, and develops into the person she was born to be. You are not alone. Thousands of parents like you wonder each day: *Will we be able to provide the resources needed to nurture our child's exceptional gifts? Will our child be accepted into special school programs that we know will be good for her? And if accepted, will she be treated like the others, based on her intellect and not the color of her skin? What happens if our child has an opportunity to go to a specialized program and we can't afford it? If I am a single parent or I live on a limited income, can I really help my gifted child?*

The results of research with families of gifted children help to give us that much-needed hope. Recent studies of Black gifted learners, in particular those from low- to middle-income families, have shown that parents can very successfully contribute to their child's achievements by using what they have readily available each day—their love, concern, and the intergenerational values that have enabled their families to be successful through difficult life circumstances. These studies confirm what we have known all along—that the most important source of our children's success, or lack thereof, begins in the home and community.

Members of the Black community have had to work hard to achieve success, and even harder to maintain it within the broader community. To do this, they invested many long hours and late nights, nurturing their children and youth throughout the generations. While it may have been difficult, they were able to do this whether or not they had additional resources or financial advantages. Teaching the value of an education, focusing on academic achievement, explaining the importance of racial pride and individual power, and utilizing the support of extended family members, like grandparents, aunts, uncles, and cousins—these are the sources of "capital" that have been as powerful as, and in many cases even more powerful than, economic capital for generations of Black families. And because others before you were able to do it, you know you can do it as well.

The Family's Role as Nurturer and Encourager

Gifted children demand lots of time and energy. They may talk almost constantly and ask strings of questions, and they are very excited about their ideas. Sometimes they keep their parents up late at night discussing thoughts and concerns and seeking advice. As they grow older, they may continue to seek your wise counsel in life matters and important decisions. You might also be the first person they want to share great or grave news with. Raising gifted children is exciting, but it also can be stressful. Be prepared!

Many gifted adults name their mother as the most important contributor to their success in school. Their mother was the family member who spent time with them talking about school-related activities; she was the one they could count on to encourage them when they felt overwhelmed by the hard work of being involved in gifted programs, enrichment, and advanced classes. Some students go so far as to say that their mother is "like their best friend."

However, fathers of Black students are also vital to their children's success. Fathers are often the "go to" parent for stu dents when they need advice on making tough choices. Students appreciate the discipline and guidance of fathers who are nurturers but who also help them focus on being responsible. Although mothers often seem to be more understanding, fathers are frequently the ones who set the boundaries, which for some students are very important in helping them make good decisions.

Black teens are faced with numerous choices every day—as are most teens—and the decisions they make are often impacted by the conversations that they have had with their mothers and fathers. Even seemingly innocuous topics, like deciding what is appropriate clothing to wear, are subjects parents can weigh in on. Choices about schoolwork, combating teasing by other students, and social matters should be among the daily conversations that your family has around the dinner table. Providing an "open forum" for discussion will make it easier whenever challenging issues arise. For example, one topic that may come up is the "sagging pants" debate. This clothing style among young Black men has caused a stir within communities nationwide. As a parent, you are in a better position to influence the kinds of clothes your son wears than anyone else. Train your son early that it is appropriate to wear a belt (that's why pants have loops) and to pull his pants up to his waist so that other people don't see his undergarments. Point out the recent article in *Ebony* magazine on the new "appropriate attire policy" of the all-male Morehouse College in Atlanta. Morehouse is known for its high academic standards and for the achievements of its graduates, who include such iconic figures as Dr. Martin Luther King, Jr. Becoming a "Morehouse Man" carries with it great distinction and honor, and Morehouse Men adhere to the college's dress codes, which do not include sagging pants. Thus, teaching your son to dress appropriately as a youngster will better prepare him for transitions to college—even if he doesn't attend Morehouse—and, later, to the workplace. Studies show that in schools where students are required to wear uniforms, discipline is better, there are fewer cliques, and students' grades improve. Although there is tremendous pressure for teens and young adults to fit in with their peers in the way they act and dress, your goal as a parent should be to maintain standards that will allow your child to progress through life with the best chances for success possible.

Parents are the most influential adults in a child's life. However, the role of the extended family cannot be underestimated. Grandparents are an invaluable resource for gifted children. As a parent, you may be the one your child comes to for advice on important, life-changing decisions; if grandparents are available, though, you may want to have your gifted child seek wisdom and advice from them as well. In some situations, grandparents can be the source of the best advice, and your child may prefer talking with them over you. Grandparents often have good stories about growing up and using one's gifts and talents, and they can also be a stable force in what can be a turbulent childhood. Sometimes these grandparents live in our homes, sometimes in the community, and sometimes across town or out of state. Even from a distance, though, grandparents are important to gifted children. In fact, it is not unusual to find them acting as parents once again and raising their grandchildren themselves; some of you who are reading this book may be in a similar situation.

Aunts and uncles can also play a significant role in the lives of gifted young people. You may have sisters or brothers who have been successful or who have done interesting things and are able to share their experiences with your children. Students often speak of aunts and uncles who have led fascinating lives—who have perhaps traveled and have had exciting experiences that they can share with their gifted nieces or nephews. If you have siblings who have the resources and extra time to spare, invite them openly to assist you with the massive responsibility of raising and nurturing your gifted child.

Gifted children and their siblings can form a bond and become another source of important, intimate support for one another. The level of understanding that brothers and sisters have for each other can be quite special. Most often, when there is one gifted child in a family, there is another, or even a third. But sometimes only one child in the family qualifies as "gifted." Be sure that the other children do not feel neglected as you spend special time, energy, and resources on the gifted child. Distributing your time and family resources among all children may be difficult but it is very important. In the book, *A Parent's Guide to Gifted Children* the authors recommend that parents spend "special time" with each child every day, even if it's only for five minutes (Webb, Gore, Amend & DeVries, 2007). This helps all children in the family know that they are important and valued. Special time with each child also helps build strong relationships within the family, which in turn helps children build healthy relationships as they mature. Healthy adult relationships with peers and others begin at home in childhood.

To many of us, "family" means everybody who helps with the raising and supporting of our children. This could mean grandmother, grandfather, auntie, an older cousin, or even someone from a neighborhood program or church. Colin Powell, former U.S. Secretary of State, remembers his neighborhood and the many "aunts" who looked after him and kept his behavior in check, remarking, "The Internet is nothing compared to the Auntnet of the South Bronx." Today, even though neighborhoods may be different, some communities still have those strong and passionate mothers, neighbors, and aunties who may not live with us but who really are a member of our "family"; these "yard moms" look after and sometimes even discipline whatever kids are in their presence.

No matter the relationship—parents, grandparents, aunts and uncles, siblings, neighborhood matrons—strong, positive family relationships are the single-most important thing we can do to ensure that our gifted children will grow into healthy and happy adults.

Family Stories and How They Can Help

A great tradition within the Black community is storytelling—sharing stories that have been passed along through generations of how family members succeeded during challenging times. These stories establish family traditions and often reinforce how important it is to get an education, share one's gifts with others, and hold true to family legacies of hard work, perseverance, and task commitment. All families have stories they can share that will help nurture and encourage gifted students' understanding of the value of education.

Talk about education with your children and share success stories of family members who have overcome challenges, beaten the odds, or been a "first" in their area of interest. Tell your children about your family history and genealogy, about family members who were the first to get an education and then reciprocated by coming back to the community or even taking on the responsibility of ensuring that others would receive an education as well. Listening to family stories gives gifted students a sense of belonging within a wider circle of individuals, and it helps them to know about others who have already passed through experiences that they have yet to face.

In addition to your family's stories, help your children find biographies of Blacks throughout history who have overcome odds to achieve and make contributions to society through their perseverance. Look at the books recommended in the appendices of this book and ask the librarians in your local library for help in finding books to inspire your children.

As your children read and hear about people like themselves accepting and overcoming challenges, they become stronger and more able to face the difficulties that they may encounter in situations in which they are the minority, in gifted and advanced academic programs, or in other arenas. Knowing about others who overcame hardship helps give them the motivation to achieve. Many Black gifted learners explain that they are driven to succeed to show the larger community that they, too, have exceptional potential, no matter what the environment looks like.

The Importance of Family Values

What values are you teaching your children? As a parent, you will set the pace for what your children believe and live by in their world. This means that you will share with your children what you believe in, what values you hold near and dear to your heart, and what values you believe will be most important to them as they encounter challenges in life. How important are honesty, trustworthiness, and respect in your home? How do family members express love and caring for one another? How do you share meals and dinner time? What are your beliefs and practices for sharing the responsibility for chores? For hard work? For leisure time? What about the type of language spoken in your home? Money and material things? Taking care of the things you own? Church attendance and religious beliefs? And education?

Answers to all of these reflect your value what is important to you. Values like these are what prompt parents to tell their children, "Remember where you came from!"

As they mature, children develop their own personal value systems from the basic values they have experienced in their home growing up. They may accept or reject the values of their parents, and sometimes they develop new values, but the values of their childhoods generally stick with them. Many parents want their children to be more successful than they were. They hope their children do not have to struggle as hard as previous generations did to achieve a good life. To guide their children, these families spend many long hours discussing and modeling the core values of hard work, dedication to task, persistence, and the importance of "giving back," or reciprocating. These are values that successful families often pass on to future generations.

The Values of Hard Work and Resilience

One of the biggest mistakes parents can make with gifted learners is to protect them too much from the challenges of life. Parents should remind themselves that children don't learn resilience if everything is easy for them. They learn persistence and resilience only when they are challenged and when they fail. We have to let them fail and make mistakes now and then so that they learn to pick themselves up and try again.

As a young girl, Katherine Johnson loved mathematics. Because she was a Black female growing up in a field dominated by White males, Katherine was not able to access the types of jobs that were of interest to her in mathematics. However, as a young woman, Katherine took a job as a teacher first and then later at NASA working with other females working on computers. Katherine's gifts in mathematics were soon noticed by the NASA administration. As a result, Katherine became involved with the team of scientists who worked on space missions. To read more about how Katherine persevered after having been discouraged, see one of the two books in the appendix about

Katherine's life story- "Counting the Stars: the story of Katherine Johnson, NASA Mathematician," and "Hidden Figures". Stories of successful individuals who have made great contributions often describe those persons as having made it despite great odds against their success. Parents should encourage their children to try out new ideas, try again when they fail, and learn from their mistakes. Failure and mistakes are not terrible catastrophes; they are a necessary part of learning. Parents can talk about mistakes that they made and what they learned from them, so children learn that mistakes, setbacks, and failures are a normal part of life and learning. Then when we master a new skill, there is a wonderful feeling of accomplishment. The wait is worth it. The struggle is worth it. We feel proud. The success after many tries carries over to the next challenge as we learn that failure is a part of succeeding.

As a parent, you want teachers and other school staff to recognize your child's gifts and talents so that she will begin participating in special programs for the gifted. However, such recognition begins with the child's achievement. Some school personnel (and parents, too) think that the child should be successful in every endeavor if she is truly gifted. This type of expectation places an enormous burden on your child and on you as a family. Others will understand that children should not be expected to be equally gifted in all areas. Most gifted individuals have strengths in some areas but not in others. You will need to assure your child that her best effort is enough; she is not expected to be perfect in every area.

You may be tempted to help your child with school projects and assignments to ensure that the work is done properly and that it maintains high standards. But when parents intervene and complete a student's work, it causes children to become dependent on others to do what is theirs to accomplish. In your well-meaning effort to help, you could be taking away your child's most valuable learning opportunities—the development of independence, the experience of being challenged by work, the opportunity to discover his own strengths and weaknesses, and the chance to learn the values of hard work and persistence. These values can only be learned when children and youth are challenged beyond their comfort level, such as when they work to accomplish a difficult task, research a problem, or discover a new idea or solution. Through this hard work, these youngsters push themselves beyond previous boundaries.

I believe that our greatest leaders would say that their most challenging obstacles have also been some of their best experiences in life—to walk a path that others have not walked or to find success after repeated attempts. Your role as a parent is to allow your child to have the same valuable opportunities on her way to becoming the person she was born to be.

In a study of more than 100 gifted individuals, researchers found that it was the encouragement of parents, teachers, and others that kept students from getting distracted, increasing their chances of excelling in their areas of talent. When your child is ready to give up because a task is too hard, the best advice that you can give him is to try again. Remind him of the numerous efforts made by successful inventors and famous Black men and women who were the first of our race to succeed. Most of the world's significant contributions to science, literature, civil rights, and the arts have been made by people who believed in the value of hard work, persistence, and resilience. Even when they had setbacks, these individuals were able to rise to the challenge and complete work in a memorable, significant way. Recommendations for stories of inspiration are listed in Appendix D of this book.

Values like persistence and hard work can come not just from the stories we read, but also from the stories we tell. Tales of hard-working, successful family members can motivate your children to work through problems on their way to achievement. I also recommend sharing a personal narrative of how you overcame a challenge, even if your child sighs and rolls her eyes. This kind of personal sharing helps build trust in your relationship. Your child learns that you faced difficulties, too, that you aren't perfect, and that it's okay to be imperfect.

Note from the author: One of my most remarkable experiences as a local school district gifted education director was a meeting held with the mother and father of an elementary-level student attending a full-time center for gifted children. The parents had requested the meeting because they were concerned about their daughter not being challenged in her classes. The reason for their concern? She was receiving all A's on her report card. The father told me how he discussed school with his daughter, and she told him that she enjoyed it, but the work was "not that difficult." Both parents wanted their daughter to be challenged in her coursework, even if it meant getting lower grades. They wanted her to learn early in life that in order to learn new material, she would have to work hard and sometimes make mistakes. I remember coming away from the meeting feeling so proud of these parents for their deep and sensible concern—not only for their daughter's present school experiences, but also for her future. In the end, the school principal made adjustments in this young girl's class placement and offered other options for extending her learning experiences.

The Immeasurable Value of Family Involvement

Some parents might want to try using "challenges and obstacles" quotes from well-known Blacks, found in Table 3, as conversation starters. You may want to post these quotes in conspicuous places or create wall posters of them to hang throughout your home. Some of them might encourage your gifted child to look at his own experiences differently.

Table 3. "Challenges and Obstacles" Quotes

Quote*	Author (with mini-bio)
"The ultimate measure of a man is not where he stands in moments of comfort and convenience, but where he stands at times of challenge and controversy."	The Reverend Dr. Martin Luther King, Jr.: civil rights leader; Baptist minister; Nobel Peace Prize winner (youngest man to ever receive the award); advocate of non-violence; first Black to have a national holiday in his honor
"Mistakes are a fact of life. It is the response to the error that counts."	Nikki Giovanni: poet and author; University Distinguished Professor at Virginia Tech; first recipient of the Rosa Parks Woman of Courage Award; celebrated by Oprah as a "living legend"
"Believe me; the reward is not so great without the struggle."	Wilma Rudolph: athlete; first American to win three Olympic gold medals in track and field; inducted into four different athletic halls of fame; named one of the Top 50 Greatest Sports Figures of the 20th Century by *Sports Illustrated*
"My mother would look at me and she'd say, 'Kamala, you may be the first to do many things, but make sure you are not the last.' That's why breaking those barriers is worth it. As much as anything else, it is also to create that path for those who will come after us."	Vice President Kamala Harris: First female, first Black & first Asian to serve as Vice President of the United States. VP Harris is also an accomplished legal scholar, having served previously as the Attorney General of the State of California
For their is always light, if only you can see it; if only you can be it	Amanda Gorman: author, poet, inspirational speaker; 3e; youngest poet laureate to speak at a Presidential inauguration

Quote*	Author (with mini-bio)
"I've missed more than 9,000 shots in my career. I've lost almost 300 games. Twenty-six times I've been trusted to take the game-winning shot and missed. I've failed over and over and over again in my life, and that is why I succeed."	Michael Jordan: recognized as the most famous international athlete of the 20th century; winner of two Olympic gold medals; inducted into the Basketball Hall of Fame; ranked #1 in the Top 50 Players of All Time (SLAM Magazine) and #1 in the Top 100 Athletes of the 20th Century (ESPN); businessman and owner of the Charlotte Hornets NBA basketball team
"Making your mark on the world is hard. If it were easy, everybody would do it. But it's not. It takes patience, it takes commitment, and it comes with plenty of failure along the way. The real test is not whether you avoid this failure, because you won't. It's whether you let it harden or shame you into inaction, or whether you learn from it; whether you choose to persevere."	Barack Obama: 44th President of the United States ; lawyer; author; 2010 Nobel Peace Prize winner; first Black President of the United States
"Presumption should never make us neglect that which appears easy to us, nor despair make us lose courage at the sight of difficulties"	Benjamin Banneker: scientist, mathematician, astronomer, and inventor (recognized as the first Black to become famous for mathematics); taught himself literature, mathematics, and astronomy; at the age of 30, he constructed a wooden clock without ever having seen a clock before, developed an almanac, and constructed an ephemeris (astronomical table that gives the positions of the celestial bodies throughout the year)

These quotes were retrieved from www.africanamericanquotes.org.

Spirituality and Black Gifted Children

High sensitivity and transcendent behaviors as related to religion have been identified in gifted individuals as *spiritual giftedness*. Children, adolescents, and adults recounting their responses to religious experiences often describe visions of angelic creatures. Numerous studies of young children report conversations during which these children reveal having seen angels, which they often include in their drawings. Do not be surprised, then, if your highly sensitive, gifted child seems to have a connection with a higher dimension.

Black religious traditions have been such a part of who we are that they are not just a Sunday experience. Black families openly discuss religion and its importance to a person's life success. In a family impact study, "moral-religious emphasis" was a theme that came up during conversations with most of the families of successful high school gifted students. One mother shared that she prayed for her children every day before they left for school. Another mother said that her children understood her directive that: "If you live in this house, you go to church." Two students spoke about the "church family" as being an extension of their immediate family. In an extensive study of relationships between Black children and the church, Wendy Haight, Ph.D. found that the children's interactions within the church were crucial to the development of their confidence and self-esteem. (Haight, 2001)

Some predominately Black churches (particularly those in the Black Southern tradition) engage in religious services in a very emotionally intense manner. These lively religious traditions are historical to the Black culture in this country and are a part of our legacy. Blacks are well-known for having ministers who are some of the most exceptional orators of any religious group. Their fervent and passionate sermons are complemented with gospel music, which has its roots in the Negro spirituals of the 18th century and has since become one of the most popular contemporary musical genres of the day. Sometimes the music is accompanied by the playing of instruments such as drums, pianos, congas, tambourines, or horns.

The "call and response" tradition—in which the minister speaks and the congregation responds throughout the sermon—is also unique in Black churches. For those visiting our churches, this is a very new and different experience. Recently, my undergraduate students in a diversity education course, most of whom were Catholic, were asked to participate in a diverse event with an organization or institution and write about their observations. Many of the students chose to attend a local Black Baptist church. Their comments about the differences between their experiences in the traditional Catholic church versus those in the Baptist church were very similar across papers. They used words and phrases like "lively," "emotional," "loud," "lots of singing, dancing, and embracing," "people moving about during the service," and "people responding out loud to the preacher." All of these comments were written in a positive manner—the majority of students enjoyed their experience, and some mentioned that they would be going back to that church again in the future, mostly because they felt welcomed and comfortable in the livelier, more emotionally expressive environment.

In many Black families, the practice of religion and the development of spirituality in our children are as natural and traditional as the family itself. For families with gifted children, it may be in church that your child's unique gifts and talents emerge. You may notice early on that your son, for example, responds at a very high level of understanding to church activities or experiences. Perhaps he analyzes the Sunday sermon or reacts in a highly sensitive manner to music, prayers, and mention of individuals in the community who may be in need, suffering from illness, or have other personal struggles. He may show early indications of high intelligence through his ability to pray or read and interpret scripture, or he may share his leadership abilities by serving as a worship leader or in youth ministry experiences.

While all children may discover an affinity for these types of experiences, gifted children are more likely to engage in them independently. However, gifted children are also more likely to question conventional religious beliefs and practices. Because of their intense need to understand and their idealistic desires, these children may question behaviors, actions, and decisions in the church that appear to be insincere, pretentious, hypocritical, or simply don't make sense, and they may challenge traditional practices. If your child does this, listen to her concerns, discuss what she has experienced, and help her to make thoughtful decisions about what she knows and believes. An authoritarian approach of "You have no right to ask such things" or "Don't question the preacher!" is not likely to work and usually drives a wedge between parents and children. Even though you may disagree, keep communication lines open, and nurture your relationship with your child. This questioning is a part of her search for truth, and many children go through periods during which they drift away from religion for a while but come back to it later.

Keeping your child spiritually connected will be important to his survival in a world that may discourage him simply because of who he is, without any consideration for his potential. Encourage your child to draw on all resources, including his spirituality, to keep him motivated and "shored up" throughout his lifetime as he works toward reaching his full potential.

Conversations with Your Gifted Child

Parents have always known that it is important to have good conversations with their children. Today, we have new educational research, as well as brain research, to support the value of talking with our children from the time of birth. Although this might seem like an easy thing to do, the fast pace of today's world can make it difficult, with distractions from all sides getting in the way of good communication. Television, computers, cell phones, and texting often become barriers to relationships within the family. Keeping communication constant and open is even more difficult if both parents work and there are several children in the family. Nevertheless, it is extremely important. Think about how little time you spend actually talking with and listening to your children. It is easy to let distractions interrupt and interfere. Yet the data show that children whose parents talk with them frequently are more likely to be successful in school. In addition, "language-rich" home environments are linked to reading success and school achievement.

Research on high-achieving Black students and their parents examined the types of activities that family members engaged in together. According to the students, family discussions and activities were integral to their school success. It was important to these children that their families were close, and the family discussions contributed to their confidence and sense of support.

Successful Black students also describe how important it is that their families talk about schoolwork and the value of education, and research confirms that a close relationship with at least one person within the family (mother, father, grandparent, or other relative) encourages the development of talent. Spending time talking during meals, during time at home, and while participating in recreational, cultural, and religious events together not only communicates your values and expectations to your child, but it also allows your child to reflect back to you how she feels about these things as well.

Sometimes, however, even with the best of efforts, your child does not easily engage in family conversations. Be patient, and keep communication lines open. You can't force someone to communicate with you, but you can create a climate in the family that fosters communication. With sensitive and intense gifted children, this can sometimes be a challenge, and you will want to make sure that sarcasm and ridicule are not part of your family's pattern because they will surely hinder communication. Be careful, too, that there is not too much criticism, particularly of your child's opinions and feelings. For the extremely sensitive child, disapproving comments can feel like an attack, and most children will be reluctant to share their ideas and emotions if they feel that they are opening themselves up to harsh critiques and deprecation. You can find many other ways to enhance the family atmosphere for communication in the book, *A Parent's Guide to Gifted Children.*

Watch, too, for signs that your child may be facing difficulties at school, such as low grades or sudden changes in extracurricular activities.

Behaviors often communicate more than words, and changes usually signal that something is wrong. Perhaps your son, being an excellent reader, is being teased or bullied at school by other students and now claims that he no longer enjoys reading. Or maybe your daughter, who really likes science, is discouraged from participating in the science fair because many of her girlfriends have chosen not to participate. Sudden changes in behavior, work habits, clothing, and attitude signal that something has happened, and at these times, a private conversation is best. Don't push or prod, but gently and sensitively find out what may be going on. Be careful not to take on the role of "the police;" remember, you are the parent, and your child needs to be able to confide in you without fear of judgment.

Also, if you have a history of confronting teachers to address your child's concerns at school, your gifted youngster may prefer that you let things work themselves out rather than having you openly come to school again. In these cases, you may want to quietly and confidentially speak with the teacher, a guidance counselor, or an administrator and ask them to intervene for you. Be sure to follow up to ensure that the matter has been addressed.

Gifted children have ideas and concerns that extend in far greater depth than most other children, and they need someone to talk to who will listen. Unfortunately, the school setting for some Black gifted children may lack a listening ear, so your role as a listener and encourager is extremely important. The following comments are from successful high school students who credit their school achievement at least in part to a strong and supportive family:

○ *My mother is definitely my rock. Ever since I began school, she's supported and pushed me. When my performance started to digress, she knew the right things to say and do to motivate me. She never stops offering to help in any way she can.*

○ *My family and I talk a lot to each other. We eat dinner together Most of the places we go, we go together. We sit down and discuss things openly so our parents can make sure that we're living according to their expectations.*

Discussing important issues with your children on a day-to-day basis strengthens your relationship, so be sure to spend time talking with your children as often as possible. Listen to their dreams and share yours with them. But above all, help your children to understand that you are always there to listen to them and to help them when they need it.

Keeping Your Gifted Child Fully Engaged

One key to nurturing and developing your child's gifts is *engagement*. Being fully engaged means that your child is regularly involved in a variety of learning and enrichment experiences at home, in the community, and at school, with opportunities to interact and share his understandings with others. This can encompass activities such as working on creative projects, practicing skills or talents, or playing and exploring outside with friends or siblings. Other types of engagement activities are more subtle. They involve developing strong relationships with family members and others who can provide positive and realistic advice on how to be Black and gifted in a majority-culture world.

Engagement also consists of solitary activities, during which your child has time alone to think about new ideas and reflect on past experiences. Having "alone time" is a challenge in today's society, though. Technology is advancing every day to keep people connected through such devices as cell phones, email programs, and social networking sites. One way that parents can validate the importance of alone time is to model solitary activities such as reading, writing, or creating artwork.

Another strategy might be to create a "shut-down" time within the family schedule. When I was a young art teacher working at the same school that my children attended, we all came home together in the evenings. To allow myself time to rest and relax after work, as soon as we walked into the house, I'd announce, "Okay everyone: Go to your own space and be quiet; it's shut-down time." During this time, the children knew that they could take a nap, read a book, or write in their journal. The only rule was that there be no noise and no equipment turned on. Today, this translates into not turning on the computer, no video games, no Wii, no Ipods, no cell phones and texting—only downtime, when everyone can appreciate the silence and time to rest as they desire. This time created in my children an appreciation for individual space and the value of solitude, encouraging them to learn how to entertain themselves without electronic devices. It also allowed all of us an opportunity to be rejuvenated before we began our evening activities. So, while engagement is important to continue motivating and nurturing children's curiosity, solitude and quiet also has its place.

Raising gifted children is a true challenge. Sometimes they are so busy and active talking, creating, working, reading, playing, and being involved in multiple activities at once that families can hardly keep up with them. These children, especially as preschoolers, are usually self-motivated and need little guidance from others to keep them engaged. Some gifted children and youth, however, particularly older children and teens, need to be gently pushed to develop their gifts.

As a parent, one of your tasks is deciding what to do to keep your children fully engaged. If your children are thoughtful and reflective and tend not to become involved in many activities or associate with other children, your challenge will be to create opportunities that will encourage their involvement. Here are a few ideas for engaging your children's mind, body, and spirit:

○   Be sure that your children read frequently. Research shows that students who read more perform better in school, score better on tests, and in general are more successful in school and college. Set aside reading time *each day* after school during which everyone in the family reads—not just the children.

○   Encourage time at night before bedtime to write in a journal. Journals provide excellent resources for self-reflection and the development of self-esteem. As a side note, your children's journals should be private. As they reach the pre-teen and teen years, mutual trust between you and your children will be important. If you have encouraged open communication with them from a young age, you should continue to have a mutual trusting relationship when they are teenagers.

○ Provide materials at home for experimentation for your "budding scientists." Even if you live in an urban area, provide a place for children to raise plants and take care of animals. This nurtures their curiosity, teaches responsibility, and enables them to express their more vulnerable, sensitive self.

○ Regularly involve your children in fine arts experiences (music, theater, dance, visual arts). The fine arts will increase their sensitivity to all cultures and enhance their creativity. Take one day a month as "arts day"—go to a museum, listen to a concert on the radio, attend a theater performance, view a public television performance, or even create a performance at home. Display children's artwork and poetry throughout the house.

○ Engage children in community service and volunteerism to nurture their sensitivities for others and teach the value of reciprocation. Teach them to respect people of all races and economic situations. Encourage them to understand that "to whom much is given, much is required," so that they are willing to share their gifts with others.

○ Gifted children often have a strong sense of spirituality. In the Black community, faith-based experiences have historically been connected to our education and success in accomplishing goals across many fields. Recognize that your children's sensitivity and curiosity is real. It may lead to questioning conventional religion; it may also lead to a desire to participate more fully in church-related activities. Strong spiritual development increases self-esteem, tolerance, humility, and patience. Keep an open mind and have regular discussions about spiritual and moral issues.

○ Create opportunities for your children to engage with children of similar abilities and interests by attending or organizing community competitions in public speaking, chess, word games, building with Lego sets, art, music, etc. This will bring students from surrounding areas together, helping your children understand that there are others like them in the community.

○ Physical activity should be a priority. A healthy body will nurture healthy mental development. Nutritious food, exercise, and recreational activities are important to your children's full development. If your children show unique abilities in any area of athletics, seek opportunities to work with professional mentors, instructors, or coaches who can provide training and sensible advice regarding the balance between developing the mind, body, and spirit.

The State of Flow

Creating opportunities for engagement may be a challenge at times; however, you, too, will be fulfilled when you see that your children's interest, energy, and intellect have new outlets and opportunities for development. Several years ago, a researcher from the University of Chicago, named Mihaly Csikszentmihalyi, developed a theory about high engagement. He found that when people engage in experiences of high interest, they enter a state of concentration or complete absorption which enables higher levels of production. This state of mind, called "flow," is described by highly productive artists, writers, scientists, athletes, and others as a place where they are so engaged that they lose track of time and all sense of their surroundings. Perhaps you have found yourself so pleasantly involved in a project that you were unaware of how much time had passed or that you had missed a meal. Sometimes we call this "being in the zone."

Csikszentmihalyi describes flow as being completely involved in an activity for its own sake. (Csikszentmihalyi, M., 2013). When your gifted child becomes involved in work in an area of high interest and skill, he may experience the state of flow. He may also discover that the experience itself is very satisfying—more so than praise, high grades, or a material reward. Sometimes the experience of flow may cause your child to forget basic needs such as eating or sleeping. This may mean that he neglects his homework or certain chores that he is required to do around the house. While we want our children to experience this level of engagement, your child should not be excused from his regular work or chores. However, knowing about the concept of flow will help you understand him better so that you are a little less frustrated when "just one more minute" becomes an entire evening. For his own sake (and the sake of your sanity), sometimes you will need to encourage your child to put the instrument away, close the book, or move on to another activity, even though he is in a state of flow.

Flow is a good thing. An intense and passionate involvement in an interest is important in developing one's ability. In one compelling study, the connection between brain development, "deep practice," and master coaching was indicated as the key to talent development. Another powerful research study found that becoming an expert in any area—whether sports, science, chess, or music—requires 10 years or 10,000 hours of practice. Think about the passion, dedication, and commitment that is required for anyone to spend the amount of time needed to become an expert!

A critical element of flow is an appropriate level of challenge. The work that your child does should be difficult enough to be stimulating, but not so difficult as to cause frustration. Thus, creating opportunities for your children to experience the kind of engagement that can lead to flow may be arduous and time-consuming. You will need to find activities of high interest that are at an appropriate level of difficulty for your child's skill level. In your search, you may find yourself seeking activities that you enjoy or have a particular interest in so that you can find the same level of enjoyment and reward that your child is experiencing. Just make sure that your child has time to spend on these areas of interest so that she can have opportunities to experience the sensation of flow. It just may be the key to developing the gifts that will lead her to future expertise!

In the Bible, the Apostle Paul mentions the word "gift" when he speaks to his protégé, Timothy, who is young, very bright, and full of potential to become a great leader. Paul encourages Timothy to "stir" his own gifts through self-motivation so that Timothy will be able to fully share, produce, and create in ways that will benefit him, as well as others around him. Parents, teachers, and others who come into contact with gifted children and teens should discover and then "stir up" these young people's gifts in ways that support and enhance flow and will lead them toward a positive future.

Below is an excerpt from a poem that my oldest daughter wrote some years ago. It expresses the complexity of a gifted learner's world and the need for engagement, solitude, and multiple opportunities to create:

I Am

Essentially singer/writer,
Intuitive, sensitive,
Fiercely independent,
Who loves to laugh,
Is sometimes talkative,
Yet relishes quiet,
Cherishes solitude,
But enjoys good company,
Opinionated, kind-hearted,
Virgo, vegetarian, music-lover,
Always reading, always thinking, always searching,
I am
A grateful child of the Creator
And
Singing
Is letting God
Fly out of my mouth.

CHAPTER 4

A Parent's Responsibility: Becoming Your Gifted Child's Best Advocate

I always want the best for him. I encourage him.
I feel that if I don't exalt him, nobody else will.

~Parent of gifted high school student

The Black Community Educating Its Own

Historically, the church has played a profound role as the first private educational institution for Black children. Before free public education for all was made the law of the land, the Black community took responsibility for educating its own, and the first schools for Black children were started in the basements of community churches all across the South. One such school in Southeastern Virginia was described like this in a local newspaper article:

> *At Black schools in the Peninsula and throughout the South, educators…were committed to helping their communities prosper, when newly freed men, women and children sought the knowledge long denied them by law. Despite operating on the outskirts of a society dominated by Jim Crow laws, these schools prospered through the support of the communities that considered them the anchors and centers of Black life.*

Some of these schools were supported by the Black community itself; others were financially supported through partnerships between northern philanthropists and church organizations. Today, Black children continue to be enrolled in religious or parochial schools in large numbers. The structure, discipline, and rigor of the curriculum are appealing, particularly for parents who believe that their children need more than what a local public school can provide.

During the Civil Rights Movement, the Student Non-Violent Coordinating Committee (SNCC) and the Southern Christian Leadership Conference (SCLC) designed and implemented voter rights campaigns that not only registered voters, but also provided communities with small-group and individual reading and writing lessons. This grass roots effort by the SNCC and SCLC was replicated by many other organizations throughout the South and, later, in northern cities as well. The goal was to equip the Black community with an understanding that with the right to vote came responsibilities, and a responsible citizen is a literate citizen.

For our children to succeed and thrive in today's society, they need to be educated beyond simple literacy. While these early efforts to provide for our community's children and youth were instrumental to our development as a culture, our young people are now growing up in a world that is fast paced, technologically advanced, and globally connected. A solid education is a necessity if our gifted children are to realize their full potential. After all, the gifted children of today will be the leaders of tomorrow politics, business, medicine, science, research, the arts, and beyond. Unfortunately, our schools generally don't work very hard to accommodate the needs of most gifted children, and minority gifted students are under-identified and overlooked all too often.

Gifted Education Today

Regrettably, parents can't simply trust public schools and teachers to provide gifted children with the kind of education they need. Gifted education is not mandated (required by law) on a national level, nor is there any significant funding provided for it from the federal government. Because there is no federal requirement to serve gifted children, states and school districts develop their own policies and provide whatever funding they can to meet the educational needs of their gifted students. In a time when many school districts are struggling to meet increasingly rigorous standards and yet also have decreased funding and high teacher turnover rates (which are greater in low-performing schools than in high-performing schools nation-wide), the first programs to be cut from school budgets are often those that serve the arts, health education, and gifted students. While some states do mandate a basic level of gifted programming in their school systems, others do not even require schools to identify gifted children, much less provide special educational opportunities for them. To see what your state requires, go to the National Association for Gifted Children's website (www.nagc.org) and look for the State of the States most recent report, or ask your local school district coordinator of gifted programs to help you.

Program services differ greatly from state to state, or even from school district to school district, based on funding and the district's interest in and understanding of the importance of providing a fair and appropriate education to all students, including gifted children. For some school districts, educating gifted learners is simply not a priority. The misconception that "gifted children will make it on their own" is typically the primary reason for this decision to not have or to eliminate special programs for high-ability learners. However, this concept is indeed misguided.

First, gifted children are still children. They don't have the maturity or the resources to know what they need and then find it on their own. Adults must guide them to help them find advanced work that is appropriate to their maturity level. An avid young reader may be able to read adult-level books, but that doesn't mean she is ready to delve into adult-level content. A budding young scientist may be excited by the different colors of chemicals when they burn, but supervision and guidance by an adult with knowledge in this area (i.e., a science teacher) can prevent potentially disastrous accidents from occurring because of the gifted child's drive to discover new knowledge.

Second, gifted children need exposure to school material that is more challenging than that used by teachers on a regular basis. Researchers have found that gifted students entering a grade already know 60% to 75% of the material that will be taught during that year. Without new material, these children easily become bored, and they stagnate in their learning. Teachers must be willing to provide challenging materials and assignments so that gifted children have opportunities to stretch their minds and learn how to work. If school is always easy, these gifted youngsters will not have a chance to develop study habits, time management skills, persistence, or resilience. They will glide through school until something trips them up for the first time—maybe calculus, or maybe biology, where they can no longer get by without doing homework or setting aside concentrated study time. Suddenly becoming unable to achieve in a subject can be emotionally devastating for children who are used to bringing home perfect report cards.

Many gifted students sail through their entire school careers without ever having to put forth an effort to attain good grades. When these students get to college, however, their lack of study skills can handicap them as they compete with other students who experienced a rigorous education program and learned how to study effectively. These students can come to believe that they were never really smart at all, which can be a crushing blow to their self-esteem; it can be debilitating enough to keep them from attaining their educational and career goals or even cause them to drop out of school completely.

One of your major roles as a parent of a gifted child is that of an advocate—a supporter, a promoter, a backer, someone who believes in a cause. You are already an advocate of your child's health, safety, and welfare. Now you need to add education to that list.

How can parents determine whether their child's school supports its gifted students? One way is to attend the annual open house and meet your child's teacher (or teachers). Ask if all of the children will be required to work on the same assignments or whether the teacher will differentiate tasks according to the readiness and ability level of each child. Some teachers are skilled at differentiation, allowing some students to work on basic skills, others to work on grade-level material, and still others, who have already mastered grade-level material, to complete higher-level thinking tasks and more challenging assignments. However, this is difficult for many teachers to do when they are faced with as many as 30 children of various ability levels in the same classroom.

It's good to establish a relationship with your child's teacher early in the year so the teacher knows that you are interested in your child's progress and that you will expect your child to find schoolwork interesting and challenging. If the work is too easy, gifted children lose interest. Some teachers, if they have a large student load and have not had training in how to differentiate instruction, may welcome a parent's ideas for what might interest and/or challenge a child. It will be easier to advocate for your child if the teacher sees you as a friendly supporter—someone willing to help him or her with the overwhelming job of trying to keep a classroom full of children motivated and actively learning. You might even volunteer to assist in the classroom one afternoon a week, although this may not be possible if you work outside of the home.

The book, *Helping Gifted Children Soar* by Carol Strip and Gretchen Hirsch, written for both parents and teachers, explains several ways in which teachers can differentiate instruction in the classroom by using learning contracts, curriculum compacting, cluster grouping, independent study, and more. It is a primer on gifted education and helps both parents and teachers find ways to address the needs of advanced learners, whether or not there is currently a gifted program in place.

Strip and Hirsch also offer practical tips to parents on how to communicate with teachers, stressing the importance of regularly keeping in touch with teachers as a way to monitor your child's progress. Without this two-way communication, both parent and teacher lose out on information that could be helpful. Parents know things about their children that might help the teacher provide appropriate instruction (for instance, the child has recently been reading about global warming and the loss of polar ice), and certainly the parent will want to know about the child's academic achievement and progress at school. In your conversations, convey to the teacher that you are available to help work with the child and that you are willing to offer ideas, suggest materials, and assist in finding resources if needed. This type of parent-teacher relationship is far better than one in which the teacher is afraid that the parent only wants to criticize and complain.

How important is it for a school to have a formal gifted program? One the one hand, a good and conscientious teacher can provide challenge for gifted students in his or her classroom, but it's really best if the entire school acknowledges the importance of being able to challenge its bright children, who otherwise might lose interest in school and never realize their potential. If your child's school doesn't have designated gifted programming, you can work with the school or school district to advocate for it. To do this, you will need to be familiar with the different types of gifted service options, what other schools are doing, and any state and local district policies on gifted programming. You should also be aware of your rights and responsibilities related to gifted education and advanced learner programs in public schools. To find out this information, talk to the coordinator of gifted programs in your local school district and in your state's department of education. In addition, each state has an association for gifted children which you can contact to learn more. Three very helpful online resources are www.hoagiesgifted.org, www.ditd.org, and www. nagc.org. And finally, there is a glossary in the back of this book to help you learn to "talk the talk" as a gifted education advocate.

Perhaps your child's school has no program for gifted students. It is even possible that the educators there don't believe that there are any gifted students in the school or the district. You can partner with other parents to ensure that your school district looks for and identifies students who are gifted and that it provides services to address those students' individual needs, both academic and social- emotional.

Remember that gifted students are not necessarily gifted in all academic areas, and so the same gifted services may not be right for every child. One child might need acceleration in mathematics, another might need more challenge across all subject areas, and a third might need more advanced academic work in addition to remediation in an area of weakness.

Sometimes parents and community members must actively work to convince schools (or entire school districts) to provide for the unique needs of their gifted students. These individuals research the laws in their state regarding gifted programming requirements. They talk with legislators and attend education committee hearings. They openly and boldly speak to school officials to make sure that these students are not overlooked and neglected. When parents strongly advocate for their gifted children, school districts often respond with additional services. The benefit is that when you speak up for your child to enact changes in the school's gifted programming, other children will likely benefit as well.

Parents wishing to learn more about advocacy and starting a gifted program can refer to the books *Building a Gifted Program* by Monita Leavitt and *Academic Advocacy for Gifted Children* by Barbara Gilman. The first book contains a PowerPoint presentation for parents, teachers, or school board members in districts where there is no gifted program or where parents want to expand services. The second book contains much helpful advice about advocacy and the importance of monitoring your child's education from preschool through high school.

How Schools Identify Gifted Students

Schools that provide special programs or classes for gifted students follow certain procedures to select which students will benefit from those programs. The identification process begins by having students nominated or referred by teachers (or parents) based on an initial set of criteria. Once students are nominated, a more extensive evaluation process determines their level of giftedness.

In the identification process, school districts frequently use multiple criteria, such as various tests and checklists or a review of student work samples, to estimate level of intelligence and potential for performance. The tools used in most multiple criteria procedures vary, but schools usually include one or more of those listed in Table 4. Most experts agree that, to be fair, schools should use several of these tools or criteria—not just one—to evaluate students for gifted program services, as gifted children do not always show their talents at all times in every setting.

Table 4. Criteria Used to Evaluate Students for Gifted Services

Tool/Criteria	Description
Parent checklist	A parent or guardian rates the child based on characteristics generally displayed by gifted individuals.
Teacher checklist	A teacher rates the child based on characteristics that the student displays in the classroom.
Work review or performance/audition	A teacher or committee reviews the student's work (usually written or project work, or live performance) using a predetermined scoring system.
Achievement test	The school administers a test which measures the student's knowledge and/or skills in academic areas usually studied in school.
Ability/Aptitude test	The school administers a test which measures a student's ability to acquire knowledge, process information, and develop skills as compared to his/her peers.
Intelligence test	A psychologist administers a test which measures the ability to acquire knowledge, process information, and/or develop skills. Scores are presented for verbal, nonverbal, quantitative, and spatial abilities, and for speed of thinking.

There are many different checklists and nationally standardized tests for measuring achievement, ability, or intelligence that can be administered by school personnel, university-level personnel, or a child psychologist in private practice. Some tests may be administered to a group; others are individual tests, designed to be administered to just one student at a time. Individual tests are usually more accurate, since they typically are more comprehensive, there are no distractions that might lower a child's score, and the test administrator can interact with the child on a one-to-one level to keep him focused and interested. High scores on achievement tests suggest potential giftedness in a specific content area. Giftedness in other areas such as art, music, dance, athletics, or leadership is usually measured through a review of work samples, portfolios, or performances judged by experts.

Gifted children show their intelligence in many different ways, and the uniqueness of each child's ability makes it difficult for schools to put into operation methods for identifying all children with high potential. You can help the school by providing as much information as you can about your child. You may want to develop a profile or portfolio to illustrate your child's abilities. A profile might include her favorite books and activities, things she does in her spare time, and how she expresses concern for others, the environment, or animals. For a portfolio, collect samples of her work from activities completed in after-school, childcare, school, church, or community programs that demonstrate her high abilities. A portfolio might contain a few original drawings, copies of poems or stories that the child has written, photographs of complex Lego building projects, a program from a music recital which lists the complexity of the piece the child played, or other evidence that showcases some of your child's gifts and talents.

Share some of the best examples of your child's work with his teacher, the gifted coordinator, or the school psychologist when they consider your child for gifted programming services. Remember, though, to avoid overwhelming educators with an overabundance of your children's work samples. A more compact portfolio with a few items demonstrating your child's unique ability will be more convincing than a large collection of many items. Information and examples from a portfolio like this can help school officials during the identification process.

Bias in the Use of Tests

While it is common practice for schools to use nationally standardized tests to measure ability and potential in children, these tests may still underestimate giftedness or high potential in Black and other culturally diverse students. As a parent, you should be aware that test bias against minority students is a concern among many in the gifted education industry. Many Black students show their potential for high performance better on tests designed to measure their reasoning and problem-solving ability (nonverbal tests) rather than on tests that measure verbal ability (tests that feature reading, vocabulary, sentence construction, grammar, and comprehension).

When school districts use only verbal tests to evaluate their students, they are not giving Black or other culturally diverse students a fair opportunity to demonstrate their full potential. One score from one test at one point in the child's life is not necessarily an accurate indicator of intelligence. In addition, if your gifted child is advanced in one area but not in others, schools that average individual subject-area scores to attain a single "cut-off" score will likely pass him over for gifted programming because the low scores cancel out the high score. Similarly, if your child is very strong in many areas but is weak in a single area which may require remediation, averaging subject-area scores to reach an overall score can mean that his weakness will be unidentified and will likely go unaddressed by the school.

Table 5 lists some of the nationally standardized tests commonly used to measure student potential and determine eligibility for gifted programs across the country. The companies that develop these tests administer them to various groups of students in different parts of the country as part of the standardization process, and they make sure that the students being tested are of different ethnic and social class backgrounds so that the sample matches the latest census data. This ensures that students from all backgrounds can fairly demonstrate their ability when taking the test.

Despite the careful development of these tests, however, different tests measure ability and potential differently, and some students will perform much better on some tests than on others. If your gifted child does not do well on a test administered by the school, ask the local coordinator of testing or the gifted program administrator which tests your district uses. You may want to have your child retested using another type of test. If the school refuses, you might wish to have your child tested by a psychologist who is well-versed in testing children. The important thing is to have an accurate reading of your child's abilities and/or potential so that you can advocate for appropriate educational opportunities for her.

Table 5. Commonly Used Ability, Achievement, and Intelligence Tests

Name of Test	Type of Test
California Achievement Test (CAT)	Group Achievement
California Tests of Basic Skills (CTBS)	Group Achievement
Cognitive Abilities Test (CogAT)	Group Ability
In-View*	Group Ability
Kaufman Assessment Battery for Children, Second Edition (KABC-II)*	Individual Ability
Kaufman Brief Intelligence Test (KBIT)	Individual Intelligence
Kaufman Test of Educational Achievement (KTEA)	Individual Achievement
Naglieri Nonverbal Ability Test (NNAT)*	Group Ability
Otis-Lennon School Ability Test (OLSAT)	Group Ability
Peabody Individual Achievement Test, Revised (PIAT)	Individual Achievement
Raven's Progressive Matrices*	Group or Individual Ability

Name of Test	Type of Test
Stanford Achievement Test Series, Tenth Edition (Stanford-10)	Group Achievement
Stanford-Binet Intelligence Scale, Fifth Edition (SB5)	Individual Intelligence
Terra Nova (CAT/6)	Group Achievement
Test of Cognitive Skills (TCS/2)	Group Ability
Universal Nonverbal Intelligence Test (UNIT)*	Group Ability
Wechsler Individual Achievement Test, Third Edition (WIAT-III)	Individual Achievement
Wechsler Intelligence Scale for Children, Fourth Edition (WISC-IV)	Individual Intelligence
Woodcock-Johnson III Tests of Achievement (WJIII-ACH)	Individual Achievement
Woodcock-Johnson III Tests of Cognitive Skills (WJIII-COG)	Individual Ability

These tests are highly recommended for use with low-income students and those from culturally diverse backgrounds.

Determining Eligibility

Once all the information concerning your child is collected (grades, test scores, observation forms, checklists, work samples), a meeting is usually held to review the information and make a decision as to whether your child is eligible for gifted programming. In some cases, an eligibility committee will use what is called a consensus decision model, wherein each member of the committee must agree with the decision. Other committees use a scoring or rating system to determine eligibility for services.

As a parent, you should know what kinds of information the committee will use to make its decision and how it will decide on your child's eligibility for gifted classes or special programs. You may even be invited to attend the meeting, although many eligibility committees only involve professionals in the decision-making process. If the committee members decide that your child is not eligible for services, you may have the right to appeal their decision. You will need to ask the coordinator of gifted services about the procedures for appeal.

Best Practices in School Options for Gifted Students

When education officials set up their school's gifted education programming, they typically try to model the methods and techniques that other schools have used that have proven to be most effective, called the best practices. Special classes and programs for gifted students should address advanced learners' needs by providing challenge, accelerating content, encouraging higher-level thinking, offering opportunities for experimentation and research, and enriching learning across various content areas. To accomplish this, gifted curriculum should:

- Emphasize higher levels of thinking and production

- Develop in students the skills and attitudes of excellent readers, writers, communicators, and thinkers

- Explore broad and complex issues, themes, and problems

- Encourage the use of diverse and advanced information sources

- Be complex and diverse, intermixing various subject areas

- Require in-depth work on student-selected topics of interest

- Provide for the development of self-understanding and the understanding of the student's relationship to other people and cultures

- Nurture creativity, enabling students to develop divergent thinking abilities, confidence, and independence of thought

- Provide for evaluation that appropriately measures higher levels of thinking, creativity, and excellence

Special Advice when Transferring between Schools

The types of services provided for gifted students can vary widely from state to state, from one school district to the next within the same state, and even within schools in the same city. Individual school districts have the right to determine eligibility criteria. If you are moving your child to a new school, you should ask the following questions: *Will they use a single test score as a cut-off score, or will they consider several kinds of information about my child when determining eligibility for gifted programming? Will they consider her grades and attitude toward learning? Will they take into consideration her leadership ability or creativity? If she was in a gifted program in her previous school district, does she need to be retested in the new school district?*

Since every school will have different answers to these questions, parents will need to get accurate information about the options available to their child in this new setting. Be sure to keep copies of all your child's grades and test scores, as well as descriptions of any special programs that your child may have participated in during his previous school experience. Providing school officials with nationally standardized test scores, letters from school personnel, and evidence of eligibility for gifted program services will make it easier for the new school district to evaluate your child's eligibility for participation in the school's programs.

Since gifted programs can vary from school to school, you should look for these elements in the materials, teaching practices, and enrichment opportunities in your child's classroom. In most schools today, teachers of gifted students must go through specialized training that enables them to stretch beyond the boundaries of regular classroom teaching. These teachers should be familiar with the options for gifted students so that they can talk about them with you.

It is important to know the kinds of gifted services available and whether they can meet your child's needs. What follows is a list of some of the types of programs and special classes that school districts may offer for gifted children:

○ *Self-contained schools for gifted children* (also called full-time centers)—all students in the school are gifted in one or more areas of study

○ *Magnet schools*—public schools with specialized courses or curricula that draw students from other school zones

○ *Charter schools*—schools that are publicly funded but which may not be subject to the same rules and regulations as normal public schools; sometimes these schools offer a more rigorous curriculum or specialize in a subject area

○ *School-within-a-school*—all the gifted students from a district attend the same school, along with regular students, and work in advanced classes for part of the day, spending the rest of the day mixed with the other students

○ *Whole-class grouping*—students are grouped according to ability for one or all of their classes

○ *Cluster grouping*—gifted students within a grade level are all placed in the same regular classroom with a teacher who has special training in working with gifted children

○ *Whole-grade acceleration*—students are skipped into a higher grade based on their high ability and need for more challenge across all subjects

○ *Single-subject acceleration*—students move ahead one or more grade levels in a single subject area of high ability

○ *Enrichment*—the curriculum is modified or extended for gifted students, usually by adding material that allows them to explore related issues or with more advanced material

○ *Curriculum compacting or telescoping*—content that the student already knows is eliminated from the curriculum, and the extra time available is used for enrichment

O   *Pull-out or send-out classes*—students leave their regular classes for one day (or part of the day) each week to participate in enrichment or extension activities

O   *Honors/advanced classes*—classes generally for students who are interested in attending college

O   *Advanced Placement classes*—college-level classes taken in high school for college credit

O   *International Baccalaureate program*—rigorous program for high schoolers in which students must meet international achievement standards in six subject areas, which includes fluency in a second language, to earn a highly-regarded diploma

O   *Dual enrollment*—students take both high school and college classes at the same time

O   *Competitions*—intellectual, problem solving, creativity, content-based, oratorical, etc.

O   *Independent study/correspondence courses/distance learning*—courses taken outside of regular school either for personal interest or for credit

O   *Mentorship or internship programs*—placing the student with an expert or professional for the purpose of exploring and advancing a specific interest or proficiency beyond the classroom

O   *Community service*—service by students, usually donated, to foster a sense of involvement and duty to the community

There are advantages and disadvantages to each type of gifted service option. Table 6 offers a breakdown of the pros and cons of some of the options most frequently offered by schools.

Table 6. Advantages and Disadvantages of Selected Service Options for the Gifted

Option	Advantages	Disadvantages
Self-Contained Program	Students of similar ability focus on topics and subjects of interest and expertise with specially trained teachers. These self-contained schools provide excellent preparation for advanced work at the high school and college levels.	Finding trained teachers is sometimes difficult, and when funding becomes an issue, programs may be threatened. Additionally, some teachers object to losing the brightest students from their classrooms to these programs.
Cluster Grouping	Students receive instruction in the regular classroom with a small peer group at their ability level. Teachers usually have special training.	Since the teacher is required to meet the needs of all students, portions of the school day will be devoted to other students. Thus, teaching time will be divided between all ability levels within the classroom
Acceleration	Allows student to take courses at the level of challenge. In single-subject acceleration, a third grader gifted in math, for example, can be tested to see if attending a fourth- or fifth-grade math class would offer the right amount of challenge for him. Whole-grade acceleration is recommended when the student is advanced across all (or nearly all) subjects.	Some students may not fit in well socially and physically with older students. Also, scheduling acceleration may cause problems between grade levels. Teacher support is important for success. Without long-term planning and continuation, acceleration is only a short-term fix. Question to ask: What happens next year?

Option	Advantages	Disadvantages
Enrichment/ Pull-Out Program	Provides opportunities for students of similar abilities (usually elementary-level) to work on projects and lessons of interest for a designated period of time.	Being removed from regular classes highlights to other students that gifted students are different, and they may be uncomfortable with this. In addition, when students return to class, they are sometimes told that they must make up work missed. Students may feel this is unfair and withdraw from services. Most significantly, students are only given appropriate educational opportunities for a few hours per week, which is typically not enough to keep them excited about school.
Independent Study/ Learning Contract	A student may select a topic of interest and work for an extended period of time on a project under the supervision of a teacher or other professional. A contract helps define the agreement.	When credit or grades are not awarded, students may prefer not to participate. Scheduling may pose a problem with professional monitors.

For more detailed information on these options and on appropriate program services for gifted children, you may want to read the book *Re-Forming Gifted Education: How Parents and Teachers Can Match the Program to the Child*, by Karen Rogers.

Competitions, Mentorships/Internships, and Community Service

Not all gifted education happens in school. In fact, some of the best learning experiences for gifted children are ones that occur in the community, such as competitions, mentorships, or community service, and parents may need to seek out these opportunities. Sometimes, too, parents must actively advocate for them because many of these opportunities are designed for older individuals and have minimum age requirements, even though a gifted child may clearly be advanced enough to participate otherwise.

Of course, many intellectual, creative, and problem-solving competitions for gifted, advanced, and highly motivated students take place within schools, beginning at the elementary level and continuing through high school. Programs like Odyssey of the Mind, Destination ImagiNation, Future Problem Solving, and Lego Logo promote creativity and problem-solving skills. Other types of competitions are also available at local, state, and national levels in most subject areas, such as science fairs, history competitions, the MathCounts program, and chess competitions. Oratorical contests and debates are re-emerging and are becoming popular with middle and high school students. Community-based competitions may provide monetary awards or scholarship funds for pre-collegiate students. School counselors, community leaders, and professionals in certain careers are excellent sources for competition information.

A mentorship is a type of tutoring experience within which a student spends time working one-on-one with a professional or expert in the student's field of talent or interest. Some middle and high schools collaborate with community volunteers through the local chamber of commerce, service clubs (such as 100 Black Men of America), fraternal organizations, and other community agencies. Some mentor programs are designed as internships, giving students a long-term experience in a selected career. Internships provide training as well as social development, enrichment, and career awareness for participating students and are offered in some schools for credit that can apply toward high school graduation.

Community service involves special projects in which students help out in community organizations, businesses, and even the child's own school. In some schools, students are awarded points or credit for completing a set number of community service hours. Some community service programs allow students to select an area of interest (for example, students interested in natural preservation may choose to work with their local Department of Parks and Recreation) on special projects that may lead to significant change within the organization.

You are the primary advocate for your child's education—both inside and outside of school. For our children to succeed and thrive in today's society, they need advocates such as you who are willing to learn about educational options for gifted children and have ongoing conversations with educators, school policy makers, and community leaders in order to make provisions for the education of our brightest youth.

CHAPTER 5
Gifted Education in Public Schools

*The time to open doors to gifted education
and AP classes is long overdue.*

~Donna Y. Ford, Tarek C. Grantham,
& Gilman W. Whiting

You now have information that will help you advocate for your child and gain access to services for gifted learners. But how will you go about it? What will you do first?

First, you must exert what Malcolm Gladwell calls your "sense of entitlement." Gladwell borrowed this term from sociologist Annette Lareau, who conducted a study comparing middle class children and parents with those from poor environments. As Lareau's researchers studied the families, they noticed differences in the ways in which the parents talked to their children, and also in how they encouraged their children to talk with adults and to seek out information. Middle class parents, for the most part, were more likely to teach their children how to ask questions and probe for more information, even when the children were talking to adults. These families felt entitled to persist in their efforts to seek information and get their questions answered.

No matter your socio-economic status, you are an entitled person. To access opportunities for your children, you must speak up and ask for those opportunities to be made available to your family. You must also teach your children to speak out and ask questions for themselves. Being entitled, however, does not mean being arrogant or obnoxious. Don't forget the old adage, "You can catch more flies with honey than with vinegar." Treat others kindly and with respect while persistently searching for information for your child. You stand a better chance of getting satisfactory and thorough answers to your questions if you approach educators, administrators, and others in this way.

Because educational options and concerns vary depending on a child's age, this chapter presents particular issues that parents should consider by breaking them down into age groups.

Early Identification and K-3 Programming

If your preschool-age child has not yet entered school but you have noticed characteristics of her behavior at home or elsewhere that indicate giftedness, start looking now for a school that will provide optimal educational experiences for her. Perhaps she is an early reader, has an unusual proclivity with numbers, or knows more informa-tion about a particular issue than most children her age. Before she enters school, you need to talk to someone who has decision-making authority related to grade-level placement and assessment.

Call your local elementary school, make an appointment to see the coordinator for gifted services, and ask to have your child evaluated. If a gifted coordinator is not available, ask for an appointment with the principal or assistant principal. When you go to the meeting, take some of the best evidence or examples you have of your child's precocious or gifted behavior, such as writing samples, drawing or painting samples, or pages of correctly-solved math problems. If you have already had your child formally tested by a school psychologist or assessment specialist in another setting, take the test scores and a report or letter documenting the name of the test and your child's performance on it. However, many schools have policies that prohibit the use of outside testing, so be prepared for the possibility that they may disregard this indicator of your child's abilities or aptitude. (You may even ask if this policy is written into your school's local plan for gifted services; if so, ask for a copy.)

If you have had your child tested but those tests will not be used by the school, ask if testing is available so that your child can be considered for early placement in school or be skipped into a higher grade. For example, can your kindergarten child move right into second grade if he can demonstrate that he already knows the majority of the content that he will be expected to learn there? Alternatively, while he's still in kindergarten, can he attend a first- or second-grade class for instruction in just reading or mathematics?

Many schools do not formally identify gifted students until the second or third grade. This is because it can be difficult to get reliable and valid measures before this age due to the developmental spurts and lags that these young children may show. If this is the case in your child's school, you may want to inquire about talent pools or enrichment programs for high-potential kindergarten, first, and second graders.

If there are limited opportunities for your gifted child to move ahead in your local school, either because the school refuses to offer more challenge to such young children or because it simply doesn't have the resources to accommodate those who need to begin at a more advanced academic level than their age peers, you will need to investigate other options. Many school districts have an open enrollment policy, which allows parents to look at other schools outside of their neighborhood or district. There is usually no cost involved for this, although parents will need to arrange transportation for their child to get to and from the school. Parents might also consider private, parochial, independent, or charter schools, as well as homeschooling. (These options are discussed further in Chapter 6.) Montessori programs are another possibility that often work very well for gifted children because they allow the children to move ahead academically as their readiness allows.

Early Entrance and Grade-Skip Issues
Unfortunately, there is a lingering bias in schools against allowing children to move ahead of their age peers, even when they are clearly academically ready to do so. An excellent evaluation tool for children

from grades K-9 that helps to work through this barrier is the *Iowa Acceleration Scale* (IAS). This is an instrument designed to guide a child study team, including parents and several school personnel, in determining whether a child will benefit from a whole-grade skip—or in the case of a young child, early entrance to kindergarten or first grade. The team collaborates to fill out a form containing questions on various aspects of the child's development. The answers to the questions are rated and, when tallied, ultimately yield a numerical score that leads to a recommendation in favor of or against grade skipping or early entrance.

The questions in the IAS prompt the team to focus on objective factors, such as the child's ability and achievement test scores, motivation, attitude toward learning, etc., all of which are designed to take personal bias out of the acceleration question and do what is best for the child. Parents, teachers, administrators, and sometimes even school counselors or gifted coordinators each provide input, and all data is recorded and examined. Sometimes the results recommend a whole-grade skip. If this is the case, a long-term plan must be developed for the child and then re-evaluated annually. Some highly-gifted children ultimately end up skipping more than one grade, although doing so all at once is not typically recommended. Sometimes, however, a grade skip is not the right answer for a child; single-subject acceleration in the child's area of strength or other curricular modifications may be a better alternative.

Whole-grade acceleration is usually more successful when it is done early in the child's school career—before the eighth grade— and this is also when schools are more likely to consider a full-grade skip. However, if school personnel resist the idea of moving your gifted child ahead to a higher grade, even if it is only in subject areas of strength, the IAS can help them to make a more rational, informed decision, and parents should ask if their school will use it with their child.School districts throughout the United States and Canada have reported success using the IAS, and some of the bias against a full-grade skip is disappearing. A new report from the Belin-Blank Center at The University of Iowa provides a guide for educators and parents on ways to support the development of acceleration plans and programs for gifted learners.

For some profoundly gifted students, a single grade skip will still not place the child in a challenging setting, and no amount of enrichment that they receive while they remain in their regular classrooms will ever be enough. Even schools that embrace the idea of whole-grade acceleration may feel uneasy about skipping students more than one grade. But when students are so far above the norm in their intellectual abilities that a single grade skip is simply not sufficient, radical acceleration (skipping more than one grade at a time) is the only answer. Since schools often balk at this idea, and since social and emotional concerns become more of an issue when a child is placed into an environment of significantly older students, there are other options that may be better. One that parents might consider is the University of Washington's Transition School/Early Entrance Program (EEP). EEP is a non-residential program that offers highly gifted children in seventh or eighth grade a chance to enter college early within a strong support system. During their first year on campus, students attend self-contained college prep courses and then later transition into the regular university population. Programs such as this one can help to alleviate many of the fears that parents—and children, too—have about skipping multiple grades.

Periodically, we hear news reports on Black prodigies who have made amazing achievements at a young age because a parent or someone else in their support system recognized that they were gifted and provided a means for them to demonstrate their talents. Some of these students attend college early; others receive recognition for record-breaking accomplishments in music, science, sports, or other areas. But for these children to succeed, someone had to recognize their exceptional ability, and more often than not, that person is a parent. Unfortunately, it may not be school personnel. As such, you will likely be your child's first advocate as discussions regarding acceleration begin.

There will probably be people who will tell you plenty of reasons why acceleration is a bad idea for your child. They'll say that she'll be smaller than her classmates. By middle school, her physical maturity will lag behind that of her friends, who may begin to go through puberty before she does. In high school, her friends will begin dating or find summer jobs, all before she is ready to do these things. Don't give up, and don't listen to those who say that problems with size or age will certainly cause your child to suffer. According to the research, such issues are very seldom problems. Support systems within the home, community, church, and social peer groups can enable your child to feel accepted and safe while she participates in above-level intellectual settings in school. Most gifted children prefer associating with older children and adults anyway because they enjoy more mature conversations and interactions. In addition, research has shown that most gifted children who are accelerated are comfortable in the new setting, adjust well socially, and find the intellectual challenge worth any social or emotional hiccups that may occur along the way.

Elementary Programming for Grades 3-5

If your elementary-age child has already been identified as gifted and is actively involved in gifted education classes or special programs, or if he is attending a school for gifted learners, you should still monitor his progress to make sure that the programs and classes continue to meet his needs. Children who receive special programming from the school need to be re-evaluated periodically so that adjustments can be made to their educational program if necessary. Parents and educators should never simply decide upon a course of action and then proceed full throttle without pausing once in a while to make certain that the child is comfortable and happy with the special services provided, as well as whether he continues to be adequately challenged and stimulated.

Whenever a child is given special programming options, it is advisable to monitor her progress to be sure that the new work is not too difficult for her, which may require either tutoring to make up for gaps in her learning, or even, in extreme cases, removing her from the gifted program and placing her back in the regular classroom. Conversely, your child may still find that her schoolwork is too easy, and additional acceleration or enrichment opportunities should be considered so that her enthusiasm for school and learning does not wane due to boredom and frustration.

If your school is one that does not test children until they are in at least the third grade and does not provide programming options for above-level work in the younger grades, then your child has probably not been formally identified nor been given access to gifted programming. However, if your child seems bored in school or com plains about the work being too easy, now is the time to insist that your child be evaluated, including formal testing where possible. You may find that your child scores well above other students on achievement tests in reading, history/social studies, mathematics, or science. Ask your child's teacher about gifted education services. Many of the gifted programming options mentioned in Chapter 4 are likely to be found in the elementary grades. Use your sense of entitlement to be persistent, although civil, in accessing services for your gifted child.

Middle School Challenges

Children grow and develop at various rates, and some gifted students may not show their unique talents until the sixth or seventh grade. As a parent, keep your eyes and ears open for emerging gifts or talents in your child that may have been hidden or dormant before. A budding writer or mathematician may "come alive" in middle school, even though his gifts were only intermittent or completely absent earlier. As a parent of a "late bloomer," you may find that you must now begin advocating for academic challenge for your child.

Most children, however, do display characteristics of giftedness at a young age, and their parents learn to advocate for them early. If this is the case and you have been proactive in your advocacy efforts, your gifted child has probably enjoyed the benefits of your persistence by being enrolled in gifted education programming in elementary school. If you are fortunate to have found a school that provides a nurturing environment for its advanced learners—or if you are even luckier to have discovered this attribute in your own local elementary school—then your child is likely to be actively academically challenged and intellectually engaged.

Middle school is different. Many educators consider middle school the most challenging time in a student's educational career. Not only is this the time during which children begin their entry into adolescence and puberty, with all of the corresponding hormonal, emotional, and social implications, but middle schools also tend to focus more on the social and emotional aspects of development and less on intellectual pursuits. For gifted children, this can be very frustrating.

Judy Willis, M.D., M.Ed., neurologist and educator, calls middle school the "black hole" of education. Services for gifted learners at the elementary level are generally noticeable and abundant. Enrichment programs, pull-out programs, and cluster grouping are commonly provided in many elementary schools, but these services often cease at the middle school level. Elementary classroom teachers attend conferences and workshops for training in how to teach gifted students, but middle school teachers seldom get the same opportunities. Thus, at the middle school level, it becomes even more important for parents to probe and inquire about what educational opportunities are available for their gifted child, whether their child is accustomed to receiving such opportunities or is new to the idea of them altogether.

To begin, you will need to understand your middle school's grouping policies and practices. Middle school grouping patterns can create either the beginnings of a period of academic rigor and success or one of complacency and underachievement for your child. Optimally, your child's middle school will offer hands-on science classes, English/language arts honors courses, foreign language and pre-advanced placement coursework, and opportunities for students to enter science fairs, mathematics competitions, and more— all to prepare students for college prep classes at the high school level. These more rigorous classes are reserved for high-performing students, while average-ability or struggling students take regular or even remedial classes. This essentially groups students according to ability, which typically allows gifted children to work at a level that is more appropriate for their needs, as well as to share their learning experiences with others who are advanced in the subject area(s) as well.

A good indicator of a middle school's commitment to academic challenge is its science, technology, engineering, and mathematics (STEM) program. Those middle schools that provide pre-algebra and algebra courses (sometimes for high school credit) are usually interested in differentiating for their high-ability and gifted students. Many middle schools will evaluate students' elementary math scores for placement in pre-algebra or algebra as early as the sixth or seventh grade. Research has indicated that students who take algebra in middle school are much more likely to take college prep courses in high school, go to college, and be successful in obtaining an undergraduate degree. Algebra is a more advanced, more abstract math, and students who can be successful in algebra early are more likely to be able to transfer their abstract thinking ability to other subjects.

Unfortunately, many middle schools do not provide this kind of attention to their high-ability and high-potential students. When their intellectual needs are not met, gifted children can easily become frustrated and depressed. Factor in the hormonal changes that take place during adolescence, and these children have a very difficult road ahead. In elementary school, being smart likely helped them to be popular, but in middle school, it's a whole different story. Teens who are smart may be teased by others as being "nerds" or "geeks." The gifted characteristics that make them so unique and so interesting are now the source for taunting and ridicule.

Teasing hurts, and gifted adolescents often try their best to fit in with their classmates to avoid it. To do this, they may camouflage their abilities around peers. They stop participating in class discussions, and some of them begin purposely failing tests or refusing to turn in homework. Their grades drop, and their social status rises. With their brains not fully matured, these students cannot see the long-term effects of their actions.

That's where your role as a parent is very important. Your job is not going to be easy during this time. The teenage years are when most young people begin to separate from their parents and exercise their independence, which prepares them for life outside of the home when they become adults. In the meantime, though, parents may find that their once-obedient child now challenges them and regularly engages in power struggles with them. Teens can become particularly rebellious if their parents openly frown on their choice of friends, hairstyle, clothing style, music, etc. If parents also start nagging their child about his sudden poor academic performance, blaming his underachievement on these same friends, then the situation may spiral downward dramatically.

To find a way to fit in with classmates, your gifted teen may engage in completely unacceptable behaviors, which may be all the more shocking because it is so different from what you have seen from her in the past. She may blatantly disregard rules that you have established for her, ignoring curfews and even participating in illegal behaviors such as shoplifting or experimenting with alcohol or drugs. While these situations also can arise in the high school years, they generally begin when children enter adolescence in middle school.

Start now to establish and enforce limits on behavior. There must be swift, consistent consequences for unacceptable behavior. The consequences don't have to be extreme, nor do you need to argue or yell. In fact, punishment can make the situation worse and the teenager more rebellious, particularly if it is harsh and inconsistent punishment. Parents who have always set consistent expectations will continue to have good relationships with their teen. Parents who have 'left the door open' for sensitive conversations tend to have better results with their gifted teen when the need for consequences arise. Consistency and calm insistence are key. Even in the most difficult situations, remember to always keep the lines of communication open—even if your teen makes incredibly poor decisions. Remember, too, that your child is still a child who needs your love and guidance, despite repeated attempts to push you away. As the old adage says, "Hate the sin, but love the sinner."

Not all young adolescents are rebellious. Many simply try their best to carve out a place for themselves among the various peer groups or cliques within their school environment. Sometimes they are successful in finding true friends who appreciate them for who they are, but many struggle with this issue. Teens who don't fit in with peers no matter how hard they try, as well as those who simply never try, preferring instead to stay true to their own inner voice, can find themselves the victims of bullying. Middle school is a peak period for bullying, and it affects a huge number of young people. According to one study, one in three children in the U.S. is bullied.

These students often suffer from loneliness, have difficulty making friends, and in some cases are even afraid to go to school. Cases of cyberbullying, in which students use the technology to bully another student, have recently made headlines. In addition to the intensity of the bullying, the Internet affords bullies the advantage of enormous exposure of cruel remarks to other students, and a few particularly sensitive victims have even taken their own lives as a result. When teasing escalates to the point of bullying, it is time for adults to step in and take action. Tolerance for bullying only allows it to progress to damaging levels.

Black gifted learners tend to suffer more within racially mixed environments when they are the only one or one of a few in a larger group of White students. Not only are they different from their peers because of their giftedness, but they are set apart from them because of their race. In some situations, teachers and counselors can help majority-race and average-ability students respect and appreciate the differences in minority gifted learners, as they might do with any student who is different. Counseling and special school meetings focusing on equality and cultural sensitivity in the school can go a long way toward helping to establish an environment in which all students are appreciated for their unique contributions to the culture of the school.

As a parent, be aware of and sensitive to the social-emotional difficulties that your gifted child may be facing during this tumultuous time in her life. Of course, if the situation warrants it, the options of private, parochial, independent, and charter schools still exist, as well as homeschooling (see Chapter 6). It may also help to enroll your teen in summer gifted programs or other enrichment opportunities with students of similar interests and intellectual abilities, which will enable her to find true peers and build stronger self-esteem. For particularly introverted children, you may have to step beyond simply encouraging your child to participate in these activities and actually insist that she try them. Some nationally recognized programs that come highly recommended are listed in Appendix A of this book.

Parents must also remember to continue modeling intellectual pursuits to their children. Even when adolescents insist that they no longer need you or even want you around (as teenagers have been known to do!), they will see the examples that you set for them in your own responsible, intellectually curious behaviors, and they will be more likely to emulate them than they are probably willing to admit.

High School

By the time most gifted children reach high school, they are coming into their own. The student artist has developed a portfolio of work that he can present when he enrolls in special programs, competitions, and later, for college admissions. Your talented daughter, who has excelled in mathematics and science, has a shelf overflowing with awards from science fairs and other similar competitions, and she is fully prepared to take advanced courses in the local high school in preparation for entry into a prestigious college or university.

Even when high-achieving teens appear to have everything under control, now is not the time to leave your child on his own; he needs you now as much as he did when he entered preschool. When you are a teenager, it is very difficult to imagine the consequences of your actions and decisions, yet those decisions can determine the course of the rest of your life. In some communities, Black boys have difficulty imagining themselves living beyond the age of 25, and Black girls may think that their only future is raising children and living off low-paying jobs. When adolescents engage in this kind of thinking, they are potentially limiting their options for what they can do with the rest of their lives. Navigating through high school programs of study, preparing for tests, choosing extracurricular activities, and planning for college are all very important at this stage, since these are the years that will most impact a student's eligibility for college. Your gifted adolescent needs your active involvement and support throughout this high school journey.

Taking advantage of all academic, leadership, and service opportunities available in high school is the key to being prepared for college. Many high schools across the country have numerous course and program options that are regularly available for gifted students. Most large high schools offer:

○ Honors coursework

○ Advanced Placement classes

○ The International Baccalaureate program

○ Online coursework/distance learning

○ Dual enrollment (taking courses at the area college or a community college for high school and college credit simultaneously)

○ Advanced student internships

○ Independent study

Other options might include work-study programs, mentorships, and early college enrollment, in addition to students joining such recognized programs as the National Honor Society. Also, participation in band, choir, or theater productions helps round out high school transcripts—and provides artistic and social experiences for gifted students. Certainly, sports are a great way to challenge children physically and allow them to compete in healthy ways against other students, while also providing the social benefits of learning team-building and, in some instances, leadership skills.

Many districts across the country are also developing magnet schools and regional schools that focus on a specific subject area, such as music, mathematics, science, the arts, etc. If a magnet program is available in your school district, seek information early, ask questions, and be sure to complete the application process in a timely manner. If you are unclear about the application process, call the school and ask for help from a teacher, counselor, or administrator. Schools usually host informational sessions for these programs, so you will want to make sure that you are regularly in touch with the school or the school counselor to get this information. If it is possible, take time to visit these specialized programs with your gifted child.

As you seek information about or access for your child to any of these options, your local school guidance counselor may provide invaluable assistance. Guidance counselors are usually knowledgeable about programs for advanced students, both within and outside the school. They should be up to date on college preparation requirements. Get to know your child's guidance counselor. Discuss with him or her your desire for your son or daughter have every opportunity to register for rigorous coursework and participate in co-curricular activities to be fully prepared for entry into selective colleges across the country. A lack of challenging courses on your child's high school transcripts will close the door to some college opportunities.

Be wary, however, of counselors who do not demonstrate an interest in or sensitivity toward culturally diverse students. Also, watch out for those who express low expectations of certain groups of students. Many Black students have experienced discrimination at the high school level by counselors who discouraged them from taking advanced courses (such as AP and honors classes) that would better prepare them for college than regular high school coursework.

Nationwide, many specialized programs for gifted high schoolers have been criticized for their lack of culturally diverse students. Recently, the valedictorian of Hunter College High School, a Black male, expressed his concern with the lack of diversity at his school during his valedictorian speech. But why did it take a teenager to point this out? Parents and community members can be proactive in changing the "face" of all gifted programs through advocacy by attending meetings for parents of gifted children, expressing their concerns to school leaders, and insisting on equitable identification practices to ensure that the school and its programs are representative of all ethnic groups.

Talent Search Programs

Talent search programs are available nationwide for gifted children in grades 2-12. These are college-based assessment and service programs that recruit students who are high performers on standardized achievement or ability tests. Talent searches locate gifted students across the country, include them in academic studies, and many times, bring the students together for specialized instruction.

Most talent searches look for students who have scored in the 95th percentile and above on a nationally standardized test administered by the child's school. If your child meets this criterion, you may receive a letter from the school informing you of the talent search. Qualifying students then take an *above-level* test. This means that your child will take a test that is written for students who are in a higher grade to see how she compares with older students in terms of her ability level. For example, the EXPLORE test, designed for eighth graders, is taken by children in grades 4-6; the PSAT, SAT, or ACT, designed for high school students in grades 10-12, are taken by students in grades 7-9.

There is a good reason why exceptionally bright students are asked to take above-level tests. Children who score in the highest ranges on a test have often "hit the ceiling" of that test; in other words, they may be able to demonstrate a higher ability than what the test can measure. When these students are given tests that are normally used for students in higher grades, they have an opportunity to show just how smart they are. This provides a more accurate reading of the student's actual ability.

There are several talent search programs, including:

O The Center for Talented Youth (CTY) at Johns Hopkins University—Baltimore, Maryland

O Northwestern University's Midwest Academic Talent Search (NUMATS)—Evanston, Illinois

O The Belin-Blank Exceptional Student Talent Search (BESTS) at The University of Iowa—Iowa City, Iowa

O Carnegie Mellon Institute for Talented Elementary Students (C-MITES)—Pittsburg, Pennsylvania

O The Western Academic Talent Search at the Center for Bright Kids—Denver, Colorado

O Stanford University's Education Program for Gifted Youth (EPGY)—Palo Alto, California

Johns Hopkins University's Center for Talented Youth (CTY) lists on its website some of the benefits of talent search participation. Students:

O Reveal previously unrecognized abilities

O Receive statistical data about their test scores by grade

O Receive recognition from Johns Hopkins University for academic talent via certificates and state awards ceremonies

O Receive email news items for gifted students and their families, as well as updates on CTY's programs

O Gain access to CTY's rewarding Family Academic Programs

O Potentially qualify for hundreds of courses offered by CTY's Summer Programs and CTY*Online*

Perhaps one of the greatest benefits of participating in an aca demic talent search is the information that students and their parents receive about the opportunities available for high-ability students. Not only do children who participate in talent searches have access to excel-lent and rewarding enrichment programs that occur year-round, but talent search students also typically form new friendships with other students like themselves from across the country. These friendships can become lifelong bonds between kindred spirits who may otherwise feel very much alone.

Beyond the Classroom

For gifted teens, as for all teens, high school can be a time of emotional upheaval. As a parent, you should be alert to any signs that your child is experiencing discomfort or trouble in school. Introverted gifted teens may exhibit signs of depression and suddenly do poorly in school; extroverted gifted teens may become actively engaged in social activities but might also suddenly begin to do poorly in school. Both situations can stem from social issues, and both need to be addressed. The depressed child may feel left out and lonely in the socially active atmosphere of high school because of her giftedness; the active child may be hiding his gifted attributes to fit in, emphasizing popularity and social fads at the expense of academics. In either case, the under-achievement needs to be reversed as quickly as possible to keep your child on the right track toward a promising future.

Some very bright teenagers talk about dropping out of school altogether, as all too many gifted Black teens do. These adolescents are frequently suffering from anger, apathy, and a lack of interest in what the school can provide for them. Dropping out of school is a form of rebellion—a power struggle. Dealing with power struggles in high school is difficult, even if parents have established a history of setting and enforcing limits to avoid them. The best way to handle a power struggle once adolescents have reached high school is for parents to band together with other parents, family members, and teachers to find ways to reach out to these teens, while also keeping expectations high and limits firm. Our gifted and talented Black students will do themselves no favors by dropping out of school or engaging in other rebellious behaviors, and it is our job as adults to make sure that the decisions they make now don't hold them back from a rewarding career later.

As adolescents grow more independent from their parents, family relationships can become strained. Peer relationships become extremely important, and the influence of peers—for good or bad—gets stronger as children grow older. The pressures that our children face in high school today are enormous. Teens are exposed to alcohol, drugs, violence, bullying, and sexual behaviors at younger and younger ages, and they must learn early to make difficult decisions. For example, if your morally conscious son becomes aware that drugs are being sold on the school campus, he will face some tough choices. Even though he may choose not to participate, he might see friends whom he's known since elementary school "experiment," and they will likely urge him to join them. It is important for you as a parent to have open conversations with your child about these topics. Share with him that experimenting with alcohol, drugs, and sex can lead to serious and life-altering consequences. The implications for his future are enormous. Even if it seems like your teen is not listening, or that he's embarrassed or dismissive, your messages will stick with him, so such conversations are very important.

Many high schools today are dealing with problems like alcohol, drugs, bullying, and teen sexual activity by hosting informational programs and meetings for parents. You should attend these meetings and keep your mind open. Whatever you do, don't say, "My child would never do that." In the pressure of the social atmosphere of schools and neighborhoods, even students with values, respect, and a good sense of right and wrong are sometimes tempted to do things they would not normally do. If your child makes a mistake, help her to know that she must suffer the consequences but that you are still her best ally, and you will help her focus on the future—not the past. Your response to her mistakes can "make or break" her at a very delicate and frightening time in her life. Gifted teens who have always wanted to do their best often suffer deep emotional scars when they fail or feel that they've let someone down. Helping your child establish resiliency in the face of failure or tragedy because of a bad decision is one of the best things you can do.

In addition to the social and emotional challenges that come with adolescence, gifted teens in advanced classes may find that they face physical challenges from simply keeping up with all the work that goes along with rigorous courses. Some gifted children suffer from physical ailments because of study habits, multiple challenging assignments, and a heavy schedule. Sleep deprivation, eating disorders, and depression are among the serious health issues that parents should monitor. Adults can help students find a healthy balance between academic work, exercise, and recreation or community service.

Everyone in the family should be a part of the continuing support system that gifted children need. Parents should be sensitive to their teens' intensity, self-doubt, unrealistic expectations, perfectionism, idealism, and cynicism, as well as their occasional poor judgment. Adolescents need to feel nurtured and accepted during this time when life is changing quickly and they are on their way to independence. Support, sensitivity, high expectations, understanding, and frequent conversations will help them achieve their dreams.

Preparing for College

Higher education is a key to success in today's world. Of course, you need to get your son or daughter ready for college academically, but you also need to create an expectation within your family that your children will seek a college education. One very good resource is the book *College Planning for Gifted Students: Choosing and Getting into the Right College*, by Sandra Berger. Two other valuable sources of information are *Everything You Ever Wanted to Know about College: A Guide for Minority Students*, by Boyce Watkins, and *The Black Girl's Guide to College Success: What No One Really Tells You about College that You Must Know*, by Sheryl Walker.

The College Application Process

As a parent, your role in the college application process is essential. You will be instrumental in assisting your child with considering choices for the right college, locating funds for tuition, and making the final selection. Start early (possibly as early as middle school, but certainly early in your child's high school career) to give your child the opportunity to investigate and consider as many options as possible. The goal is to find a college where he will be intellectually challenged, have a positive experience, find a group of peers with similar interests and common intellectual pursuits, and graduate with a degree that will allow him to either enter his career of choice or continue toward a graduate degree.

Taking advantage of opportunities to visit colleges can get this process off to a good start. You can take a family trip for a weekend to an area college to see what the campus looks like, but be sure to schedule formal visits to at least two or three colleges so that you can get the most information. Visits can help your teenager begin to feel comfortable on a college campus and ease some of her concerns about being in an unfamiliar environment. College admissions counselors, student affairs staff, and sometimes even faculty and current students are available on college preview days or visitation weekends to familiarize your child with the campus and answer any questions. In addition, if your child has the option to attend a summer enrichment program on a college campus, try to ensure that she is able to go. Giving her a taste of the college experience early helps as she considers what careers and schools she wants to attend.

The question of whether your child wants to pursue a degree at one of our nation's many Historically Black Colleges and Universities (HBCUs) is one that you should discuss. Many HBCUs have outstanding performance records and have graduated some of our nation's greatest leaders in politics, education, science, and the arts for more than a century. These universities can be public or private and offer either two- or four-year degrees. They are primarily located in the Eastern and Southern parts of the country, so if your child chooses one of them, it may mean leaving your home state. However, your child should be encouraged to look at both out-of-state and in-state colleges, as well as single-sex education and military colleges. Many colleges send representatives to communities for "college night," during which prospective students can get more information from several colleges at once. Make sure you and your child go to these events. Being informed and considering all options will give your child the greatest chance of finding the school that best meets his needs.

Some Black families have a tradition of their family members all graduating from the same college—often an HBCU. It can be tempting to want to encourage your child to follow the tradition.

However, the decision should be based on whether the college offers a program that meets your child's educational needs and career plans. Visiting the college campus and talking with university personnel will give you and your child invaluable information to help in making the decision. Your child should feel free to choose which college is right for her without pressure from family members loyal to their alma mater.

Some Black students may prefer to attend a college campus more diverse than an HBCU. Give your child the opportunity to consider the advantages and disadvantages of both types of environments. Once your child has narrowed the college choices, perhaps he can create a chart of pros and cons that will include information such as:

○ Options for majors
○ Size of student population and approximate size of classes
○ Academic reputation of professors
○ Graduation rates for Black students
○ Affiliations with various clubs and organizations
○ Options for athletic programs/scholarships
○ Scholarships and grants available
○ Proximity to potential internships
○ Connections with major corporations, businesses, and national organizations of interest
○ International travel options
○ Housing accommodations

These are just some of the features that your child should consider when deciding which college to attend. As you discuss college selection, more ideas may surface. The guidance counselor in your child's school may also suggest other factors.

Of course, many of the options that may seem particularly attractive to college-bound adolescents cost a great deal of money. For students who get good grades in middle and high school, financial assistance is often available. Students whose grades, community service, and extracurricular experiences are exceptional will have access to a variety of scholarships and grants, so students and their parents should do their homework and learn about what is available to them. Again, the guidance counselor can help with this process, but be sure to inquire early. Scholarship and grant applications have certain requirements and deadlines for filing. Learning what your child needs to do in advance will increase your family's chances of receiving these sources of assistance. Accessing free financial aid from federal sources is also an option; this requires an annual application through Free Application for Federal Student Aid, available at www.fafsa.gov.

Popular magazines today are encouraging young Black students to go to college, and many of their articles provide websites and other helpful information to students applying for college. *The Black Collegian* is one excellent example, and its website (www.blackcollegian.com/index. php) has links to invaluable higher education resources specifically targeted for Black students.

Note from the author: When she was a high school senior, my daughter was given the option to attend the Naval Academy in Annapolis, Maryland. As a star athlete on her school's basketball team and a gifted, high-performing academic student, she was viewed as an excellent candidate for admission. Our family was very excited for her, and also apprehensive. The Naval Academy admissions process was very detailed and time-consuming, but as I look back, I realize that it was an excellent learning experience for my daughter. While she eventually chose not to attend the Naval Academy, I am sure that she will never forget the experience of preparing for admission.

To attend the Naval Academy, students are required to meet stringent academic and physical requirements. To prepare for this, my daughter had attended two summer programs in Annapolis while she was still in high school—a science camp and a basketball camp. These camps were a financial burden for our family, but we felt that they were worth it. She enjoyed the academic and physical challenges, the excitement, and experience of both programs.

As a student-athlete, my daughter was well-prepared for the physical requirements of joining the Navy; academically, she was less prepared because the offerings in our small, rural, community high school did not prepare her to be as competitive as other students. Despite taking advantage of the highest-level courses available there, the coursework was still not sufficient for direct entry into the Naval Academy. Students who fail to meet the Navy's high academic preparation standards are given the option of attending the Naval Academy Prep School in Newport, Rhode Island, for a year to prepare for the rigors of the Naval Academy. A visitation appointment was made for us, and we drove to Rhode Island from our home in Virginia.

After returning from the Prep School visit and giving her future much thought, my daughter decided not to go to the Naval Academy and accepted admission to the University of Chicago instead (she had completed and submitted her application to Chicago on her own earlier during her senior year). The University of Chicago provided grants for her entire four-year period there to lessen the financial burden for our family and make it possible for her to attend. She matriculated at Chicago, participated in athletics, performed in choir, and graduated four years later with a degree in English. The limited coursework at her high school made attending Chicago quite a challenge, but with hard work, persistence, and a great deal of family support, she excelled in both academics and athletics. During her Chicago experience, she took advantage of tutoring, held a part-time job, and limited her recreational time in order to focus on her studies. This is just one story; other young people have done the same. Your child can do it as well. Nothing is impossible.

What Colleges Are Looking for in Their Students

When making admissions decisions, college admissions officers consider many different factors. While your child's grade point average is important, colleges also look at students' transcripts to determine the quality and rigor of coursework offered at the school, as well as which courses they have chosen to take. Students who seek challenges and take higher-level courses are in a better position to be accepted to college than those who take only basic courses. Equally important is evidence that the student is a well-rounded individual and has participated in extracurricular activities, which may include leadership, sports, music and drama, clubs and organizations, competitions, and volunteerism in the community. In addition, most colleges require letters of recommendation and/or a personal essay.

When discussing college preparation with your child, be sure to talk about all of the college entry requirements. Your college-ready teen should be able to express himself well, both verbally and in writing. Some colleges, and even some scholarship applications, require face-to-face interviews. Your child needs to be prepared to respond to questions about himself and his plans for the future. Good writing skills will help your teen produce a college application essay that reflects his abilities and intelligence; they will also be necessary for high performance in his classes once he gets to college.

What Should You Look for in a College?

Campuses that have tutoring, student writing labs, and library support five to seven days a week are student-friendly environments. As mentioned previously, gifted students are not always gifted in all subjects, and they may need additional support or tutoring in one area or another to improve their chances for success. This is particularly likely if they attend a high school that provides only limited opportunities for readiness in a highly competitive college environment. Once she gets to college, encourage your child to take advantage of these university services. She should learn as early as possible how to ask for help—and not be ashamed to do so.

Some colleges offer a "bridge" program during the summer prior to a student's first year. These programs help to orient students to what will be expected of them in their college courses. Some offer introductions to college writing, mathematics, and reading comprehension courses. If your teen is invited into a bridge program to improve his college readiness, encourage him to take advantage of the opportunity, even if he is gifted. This experience can help him understand that he will need to work hard if he expects to achieve at a high level, which may not have been the case for him in his high school classes.

Most university campuses also have first-year seminar programs, which last anywhere from one semester or quarter to an entire year. First-year programs are designed to help your child become comfortable in the university environment and learn the rules, regulations, and responsibilities of being a college student.

Attending college is another stage in your child's journey toward acquiring a complete education and preparing for the future. However, your child needs to understand that being accepted into college and having the potential for accomplishment and success is not the same as successfully completing a four-year degree program. To earn a degree, even the most gifted and highly able student should seek out and take advantage of support from faculty, peer tutors, learning communities, and other university staff. Of course, your child should know that her greatest support comes from the home. Whatever challenges and frustrations she may encounter along her educational journey, she should always know that she has a a loving family who will encourage her to do her best. She should know that when she has challenges, she can to talk to her parents, older sibling, and other family members to encourage her unconditionally as she finds resolution to her challenges.

CHAPTER 6

Other Options Outside the Public School System

It starts with the premise that talent resides in every American community—and then puts that talent in the way of opportunity. It's as simple and powerful as that.

~Deval L. Patrick, 71st Governor of Massachusetts

Today, Black parents have many options for their children's education. White families are not the only ones to seek out alternatives when schools are not meeting the needs of their students; minority families too can look at other options. A growing number of Black parents are enrolling their children in independent, private, and parochial schools nationwide, and some are schooling their children at home. Many parents also work with community groups to develop charter schools using funding providing by local school districts. Additionally, Black families are taking advantage of specialized summer and Saturday morning enrichment programs that provide advanced instruction for gifted students as they prepare for accelerated programs at the high school and college levels.

It is not enough to know that you have choices, however. You must also have information about the alternatives that are available for your gifted child. This chapter discusses some of the most relevant opportunities for high-achieving Black children outside of the public school system.

Independent, Private, Parochial, and Charter Schools

The difference between independent schools and private or parochial schools is very subtle, and many people use the terms synonymously. While these schools are similar in that they are not funded or governed by federal, state, or local governments, independent schools are guided by an independent board of directors or Board of Trustees—i.e., they govern themselves. Private schools are governed by outside organizations, and most parochial schools are owned, financed, and governed by religious institutions. In contrast, charter schools are publicly funded but are not subject to the same rules and regulations as other public schools; however, they must produce certain results in exchange for this freedom. Many charter schools specialize in a certain subject area (for instance, mathematics or science), but nearly all have a waiting list. Despite their differences, all four of these types of schools were established to allow students access to a higher quality of education than what most public schools can offer.

Independent Schools

In general, most Black students who attend independent schools find great satisfaction with their educational experiences there. In fact, according to a study by the National Association of Independent Schools (NAIS), the vast majority of Black students in independent schools feel that the school nurtures and supports them and that it adequately prepares them for college and life beyond. However, many of these same students still feel some pressure to fit in with their White peers, and nearly all of them indicated that they have experienced some type of racism, although in no instance was the racism displayed overtly. The NAIS reports that only 5.9% of students in independent schools are Black, so it should not be surprising that many of these students indicated feelings of not belonging.

Despite being in the minority, Black gifted children who need more challenge should still consider independent schools as an alternative to public schooling. For resilient children who are particularly frustrated with a slow pace in their current classrooms, the academic rigor of an independent school will be immediately appreciated, and intellectual peers of any color will likely become fast friends. However, if your child is struggling to find peers who look like she does and have the same cultural history that her family has, there are other independent school options.

Historically Black independent schools include several boarding schools that were formed by private citizens and churches throughout the Northeast and South. Four Black boarding schools still serve children today. These schools offer academically enriched curriculum and small class sizes, with a focus on character building, Christian values, and the rich history of Black culture. All four schools also provide extracurricular activities, including competitive sports teams. The Piney Woods School, located in Piney Woods, Mississippi, is the oldest, perhaps the most well-known and well-funded. The other three schools are: Redemption Christian Academy in Troy, New York; Pine Forge Academy in Pine Forge, Pennsylvania; and the Laurinburg Institute in Laurinburg, North Carolina. Each of these boarding schools boasts very high success rates, with nearly all graduating students attending college.

Private Schools

Increasingly, Black parents are considering private schools to educate their children, and Black students are widely represented in Catholic schools and church-affiliated private schools operated by community boards. (Most, although not all, private schools are operated by religious institutions and organizations. Parochial schools are specifically private schools that also offer a reli gious education.) These types of independent programs are available throughout the United States.

Private schools often offer structure, small classes, rigor, and highly qualified teachers that may not be found in public schools serving students in predominately Black neighborhoods, particularly in depressed urban and rural areas. However, "private school" does not always mean "better school." There is a widely held misconception that all private schools have a more challenging curriculum and provide a better quality of education than public schools, but this is not always the case.

If you are considering a private school for your gifted child, ask about qualifications of school personnel, history of student achievement, longevity of the school's program, and special curriculum modifications for gifted children, as you would for any school. In small community or church-affiliated private schools, it is particularly important to ask about teacher qualifications, including whether all teachers have training and certification in their assigned teaching areas. You should also ask about what special training, if any, the teachers and administrators have in gifted education.

A good private school should be managed by a highly skilled administrator who interacts with teachers, students, and parents to ensure that students' needs are consistently met and that your child has access to:

○ rigorous, challenging curriculum, including opportunities to engage with professionals in the fields of mathematics, science, social sciences, and the arts

○ teachers who are highly qualified in the grade and content area they teach

○ opportunities for competitive experiences within the school and with similar schools

If you decide that your gifted child's needs cannot be met within the regular local public school, you might investigate private, independent, or specialized schools. Also, you may want to explore charter schools and magnet schools, which are public school options. Be sure to make an appointment to meet with the school's administrators. Administrators who take a personal interest in each child's success tend to operate schools with the highest achievement, graduation, and college attendance rates.

You may need to do some research on the school before you talk with the educators and administrators there. Also, you will want to factor in your child's unique educational needs. In determining whether a particular school is the best fit for your gifted child, you should consider several issues:

1. In what academic content area(s) or extracurricular area(s) does my child display strengths, talents, or special interests?

2. How does the school address students' special gifts and talents?

3. Does the school have a strategic plan to address Diversity, Equity, Inclusion, and Social Justice?

4. Does the school allow students to learn at their own pace, or is everyone expected to learn the same material in the same way at the same time

5. Does the school provide professional learning for teachers in gifted education and cultural competency?

6. What resources and materials are available to expose students to the newest concepts and developments in a variety of fields, as well as to allow students' in-depth pursuits of their areas of special interest and abilities?

7. How does the school arrange opportunities for children to be exposed to other students and adults who share their strengths, talents, and interests?

8. What speakers does the school invite to help students consider career possibilities and to cope with rapid change in our world?

9. Are opportunities for advanced content or courses provided for students whose achievement warrants them?

10. What enrichment opportunities are offered to students that expose them to experiences across all content areas outside of the school day?

11. Do the teachers use strategies that enable students to learn and apply skills in critical and creative thinking, problem solving, decision making, and teamwork?

12. How are students made aware of opportunities to participate in special programs to develop these skills (e.g., Future Problem

Solving, Destination ImagiNation, Invention Conventions, Odyssey of the Mind, Knowledgemaster, Lego Logo, pre-engineering competitions, science fairs, art shows, etc.)?

13. Do the teachers teach problem-solving skills using real-world problems to plan and conduct research, rather than relying on contrived, textbook exercises?

14. How does the school keep parents informed about student progress, teaching strategies, and course content being taught in class?

15. Do the teachers ask me about my child and discuss the insights I have about his or her interests, activities, experiences, relationships, and feelings about school, as well as in areas outside of school? How do teachers document this information?

Successful schools for Black students include characteristics of historically Black independent schools, as well as attributes of contemporary specialized schools. See Table 7 for a list of characteristics to look for when considering a school for your child.

Table 7. Characteristics of Successful Schools for Black Students*

Small class size: A smaller teacher-to-student ratio allows your child's teacher to provide more individualized assistance and use more creative teaching strategies to meet individual learning needs.
Caring, committed, culturally sensitive teachers: This means teachers who are competent but who also demonstrate that they are culturally responsive—i.e., understanding and sensitive to children's ethnic backgrounds, communities, family structures, interests, and learning strengths.
Curriculum uses materials representative of a variety of cultures: This includes visual images throughout the school—its website, brochures, books in classrooms and libraries—used year-round. These images also include both male and female role models, contemporary and historical across disciplines.

Active family/community engagement programs: Parents and extended families are regularly involved, visitation is controlled but allowed, home visits are conducted, and families are seen as partners in the educational process.

Provision of before- and after-school, summer, and Saturday morning programs: Tutorials, enrichment, content seminars, career days, etc. are provided as a regular part of the educational experience.

Black male and female role models: Teachers, administrators, community leaders, and other school staff are represented in a respectful manner and seen as role models for all children.

Integration of the fine and performing arts within the curriculum: Fine arts, including visual arts, music, theatre, and dance, are incorporated into all learning, not as a frill or extra expense. Arts legacies of all cultures are taught. Cultural event field trips are hosted throughout the school year.

Overt disciplinary policies and procedures: High standards for behavior are set and expected for all. Respect is shown, and all students are expected to be respectful. Consequences for poor behavior are known and practiced.

Service learning/community interaction programs: Teaching students to reciprocate is part of the regular curriculum experience. Community projects are designed to contribute to the greater community's wealth and prosperity. Ecologically friendly environments are encouraged, and students serve as learners as well as leaders in service programs.

High expectations, character, and integrity are noticeable throughout the environment: All personnel show and expect students to demonstrate excellent character and integrity daily. Character education training includes teachers and administrators, as well as support personnel.

Offers advanced and honors courses as early as middle school: These courses prepare for entry into advanced coursework and, later, college. Students must have access to Algebra I as early as middle school (grades 6-8), and Honors/Pre-AP English should include classic Black and traditional literature, writing, and grammar.

Academic competitions: Oratorical, science, technology, and other types of competitions enhance self-confidence and communication skills and expose students to others from varied environments. Competing team participation is a necessary part of the school experience. These competitions should also provide for summer travel and academic year travel experiences.

International travel: Opportunities should be available for travel to other continents, such as Africa, Europe, Asia, and South America, in middle and high school, perhaps through Rotary International or other exchange student programs.

*These characteristics are based on a compilation of research on successful Black independent schools, preparatory school models, alternative schools, "effective schools" research, and schools for gifted learners.

Programs Bridging the Gap between the Haves and the Have-Nots

Private schools can be very expensive, and sometimes parents find that the cost of an optimal educational experience for their gifted child is a problem. Across the country, innovative program models, supported by both private and public funding, are in place to assist parents of Black students (and other culturally diverse, at-risk groups) with educating their children. Many of these programs particularly try to assist first-generation college attendees in navigating the financial burdens of a better education by providing access to private schooling, as well as higher education.

A Better Chance

The longest running program of its type, A Better Chance (ABC) is one of the nation's first college preparatory programs designed to provide early enrichment experiences to high-potential, low socio-economic, minority youth. For nearly 50 years, ABC has provided for the educational and social needs of thousands of talented, culturally diverse students, placing them in private boarding or day schools so that they can access high-quality educational opportunities that may not be afforded to them elsewhere. These schools provide small class size, rigorous college preparatory courses, individual counseling, and cultural and social enrichment opportunities—all to prepare students of color to assume positions of leadership and responsibility. ABC boasts successful alumni who have become leaders in many areas, including Deval Patrick, the first Black Governor of Massachusetts. Visit www.abetterchance.org for more information.

Black Student Fund (Washington, DC)

The Black Student Fund (BSF) provides financial assistance and support services to Black students and their families in the Washington, DC, metropolitan area. Its mission is to increase the enrollment of Black children in independent schools and to make sure that those students' experiences are positive. BSF-assisted students in pre-kindergarten through grade 12 typically graduate from high school with distinction and then enter college. Most of these students are from single-parent, low- to moderate-income households, and many are the first in their families to progress to a higher education. Through referral programs, summer and scholarship programs, and crisis intervention programs, BSF strives to assure that Black students have equal access to every educational opportunity. Go to www.blackstudentfund.org to learn more.

Connecting Communities to UCLA (Los Angeles, California)

Connecting Communities to UCLA (CCU) is a relatively new organization that works to connect UCLA with surrounding communities to provide their children better opportunities for a strong future. Through a variety of programs and events, which are touted as both educational and fun, CCU strives to help young people see the value in attending and completing college, and work toward that goal. Programs include Females in Math and Science, Career Day, and the Early Academic Outreach Program (EAOP), which is designed to bring families, schools, and communities together to help disadvantaged students expand their postsecondary education options through challenging enrichment activities. In addition, CCU's programs enable children and teens to develop leadership skills and become involved in community service efforts. For more information about CCU's programs, go to www.ccu.ucla.edu.

Davidson Institute for Talent Development (Reno, Nevada)

In operation for just over a decade, the Davidson Institute works to recognize and support profoundly gifted children to give them opportunities to develop their talents. Profoundly gifted children are those who score in the top 99.9th percentile on IQ and achievement tests, which puts them in an IQ range above what even normal gifted programming can accommodate. The Davidson Institute offers a wide range of programs and services to help these children and teens find appropriate learning opportunities, while also providing information and education to teachers, counselors, and other professionals who work with these young people. Programs assist parents and students with academic advocacy, offer scholarships, connect interested educators with resources and strategies for serving gifted children, and much more. The Davidson Academy is a free public school that allows highly gifted students to progress through middle and high school curriculum at their own accelerated pace and then proceed on to the University of Nevada. At the THINK Summer Institute, a three-week residential summer program, 13- to 16-year-olds take college-level courses for college credit. The Davidson Institute also offers a gifted database and is an excellent source for information related to giftedness. Visit www.ditd.org to learn more.

Illinois Mathematics and Science Academy (Illinois)

The Illinois Mathematics and Science Academy (IMSA) is a teaching and learning laboratory for academically talented students in science, technology, engineering, and mathematics. IMSA offers enrichment programs for students of all ages, but those in grades 10-12 can participate in its highly competitive residential college preparatory program. IMSA also delivers professional development programs for math and science teachers, and it provides innovative instructional programs that foster imagination and inquiry to Illinois teachers and students. Go to www.imsa.edu for more information.

Jack Kent Cooke Foundation Young Scholars Program

The Jack Kent Cooke Foundation provides scholarships to youth from economically disadvantaged backgrounds who have demonstrated potential and a desire for advanced academic educational experiences but who lack the financial means. More than 600 students annually receive funding throughout high school, college, and graduate school so they can fulfill their potential and emerge as leaders in all academic areas and the arts. The Foundation's staff designs an individualized program for each student scholar, which includes summer programming and distance learning. Jack Kent Cooke Scholars not only receive funding for their education, but they are also guided and supported by a staff of advisers, and they receive mentoring from professionals and civic leaders. The Foundation also partners with outstanding educators to enable lower-income students to experience the academic challenge that they need to develop their talents. For more details, go to www.jkcf.org.

Jacob's Ladder (Urbanna, Virginia)

Jacob's Ladder is an enrichment program that follows gifted, at-risk students for five years, from grades four through eight. "Climbers" are provided school resources for the academic year and attend a four- to six-week summer camp held on the campus of a residential private school. In addition to academic enrichment, students are immersed in character development throughout the program. When Jacob's Ladder students are ready to enroll in high school, they are given the choice to attend one of several highly selective private boarding or non-residential schools in Maryland, Virginia, and North Carolina. In its almost 20 years of operation, Jacob's Ladder students have been accepted into some of the country's most prestigious colleges and universities, attesting to its success rate. For more information, go to www.jladder.org.

North Carolina Project SEED (North Carolina)

Since 1968, the American Chemical Society's social action program, Project SEED, has made research laboratory experiences available to gifted students from disadvantaged backgrounds. The eight- to 10-week summer program provides hands-on research experiences for high-achieving high school students so that they can pursue graduate and professional school degrees in chemistry or a related field. In this program, each student completes a research project under the supervision of an experienced SEED scientist in an academic, industrial, or government research laboratory and receives an educational award. There are more underrepresented minorities in North Carolina's Project SEED program who go on to become national science competition winners than in any program in the state, and perhaps the country. In addition, 96% of its students attend college, with 75% receiving full or partial scholarships. Visit www.ncprojectseed. org for additional information.

Oliver Scholars Program (New York City, New York)

The Oliver Scholars Program offers academic, social, and financial support to highly motivated Black and Latino children in New York City. The program identifies these children in the seventh grade and then provides the guidance and support necessary for them to earn admission to select independent schools in the Northeast. It then continues to support them all the way to college. The Oliver Scholars Program was initiated to provide minority children with the resources needed to help them attain an education better than what most public schools can offer. To do so, it allows culturally diverse gifted students and their families to interact with a community of supportive educators, sponsors, and peers, thus promoting social equity. It also encourages the pursuit of excellence in scholarship, leadership, and service. Go to www.theoliverprogram.org for more details.

The SEED Foundation (Washington, DC, and Maryland)

The SEED Foundation partners with urban communities in Washington, DC, and Maryland so that underserved students can be given the opportunity to successfully attend college and go on to work in their areas of potential. SEED schools combine a rigorous curriculum with a boarding school setting. This allows students to learn academic and life skills in a safe and secure environment. The goal of the SEED schools is to provide a college preparatory boarding school education to children who may not have access to this type of schooling due to their low socio-economic status. Recognized as one of eight Charter High Schools for Closing the Achievement Gap, the SEED Foundation boasts a 97% college acceptance rate among its graduates. It is currently looking into the possibility of setting up more schools in Ohio and New Jersey. For more information, go to www.seedfoundation.com.

Step Up for Students (Florida)

Step Up for Students is an initiative of the Florida Tax Credit Scholarship Program that was created to help K-12 students who live at or near the poverty level receive an appropriately challenging education, which might be unavailable in their current neighborhood schools. The program gives Tax Credit Scholarships to low-income students so that they can attend out-of-district public schools or private schools—not so much because their current public school is failing, but rather because some students simply learn better in environments that offer different methods of teaching or alternate enrichment opportunities from what they're exposed to in their own district. The money from the scholarships can be used either for private school tuition or for transportation to schools out side of the child's home district. Visit www.stepupforstudents.org to learn more.

The Black Homeschooling Movement

In addition to independent and private schooling, an increasing number of Black parents are deciding to homeschool their children. According to a recent article in The New Yorker (2021), the Census Bureau estimated that 16% of Black students were being homeschooled across the nation. There are Black parents joining together with others who are seeking to improve their children's educational experiences. These parents are also being supported by grant funds from conservative philanthropists, like the Koch foundation.

Families decide to homeschool for many reasons. Most often, parents choose this route because they believe that they can offer a higher quality of instruction, safety for their children, and a culturally relevant curriculum, which includes religious, ethical, and moral issues. For highly able and gifted children who need more than what is traditionally presented in regular school programs, homeschooling offers an opportunity to learn at a faster pace, in more depth, and with a focus on areas of their particular interest.

In a revealing memoir of her experience, one mother describes why she and her husband made the choice to homeschool their Black sons, as well as the specific strategies they used (Penn-Nabrit, 2003). Contrary to what some believe, homeschooled children tend to score higher on standardized tests than publicly educated children, and all three of this couple's sons were accepted into Ivy League colleges.

Homeschooling is a huge job, and parents should not attempt to undertake it if they don't have the time or the resources to do it. Luckily, there are many resources out there that can help. An excellent book is *Morning by Morning* by Paula Penn-Nabrit, the memoir just mentioned. Not only is it an interesting and compelling story, but it also lists many helpful homeschooling resources in the appendix. An excellent on point guidebook is *The Homeschool Alternative: Incorporating a Homeschool Mindset for the Benefit of Black Children in America* by Myiesha Taylor and Haley Taylor-Schlitz. Another book is *Creative Home Schooling: A Resource Guide for Smart Families* by Lisa Rivero. This book is a must-read for anyone considering homeschooling their children.

Note from the author: After some initial research on homeschooling within the Black community, I decided that an organization called the Black Home Educators could help me determine the breadth and depth of the experiences of African American parents who were homeschooling their children. In the fall of 2009, I requested to join, and I was welcomed into the group by its founder, Mrs. Ty Banks. I was in for an awakening! Not only have I learned that a great number of Black families homeschool their children, I have also been introduced to a group of highly intelligent, deeply passionate African Americans who make sound, efficient, and effective decisions about the education of their children on a daily basis.

To gather information about their experiences, I developed and posted an online survey. Although only 20 responses came in, I got a very clear sense of who these families are. The practices that they use in their homeschooling programs are essentially what the educational community has come to know as best practices for educating gifted children. Their specific comments demonstrated to me that they are engaging in individualized instruction, constructivist teaching (in which the student is actively involved in the learning process through a form of guided discovery), character development, and culturally relevant practices. These parents are well-educated and have made the decision to do what they believe they are better equipped to do than either public or private institutions—teach their children at home.

Here are some specific results from my homeschooling survey:

○ What are your reasons for homeschooling? Sixteen of the 20 respondents indicated dissatisfaction with public schools; eight listed dissatisfaction with private schools. Almost all also remarked upon their confidence in their ability to teach both core and specialized subjects.

○ Do you have a child who has been identified as gifted or one who is currently going through an evaluation process for gifted services? Nine of the 20 respondents said that their children were either identified as gifted or were in the process of being identified before they began homeschooling. One parent, whose son was found eligible for gifted programming, opted for homeschooling because there were no special classes at his local school for gifted children.

○ How long have you been homeschooling? One-fourth of the families had been homeschooling for one year; the rest had been homeschooling for two or more years, with three families stating that they had been homeschooling for four or more years.

O   Please describe your educational level. Half of the parents had high school diplomas with some college; 10% had undergraduate degrees; 20% had graduate degrees, and 10% had post-graduate degrees. Their content expertise ranged from education (16) to math/science (2) to professional degrees in law, medicine, or engineering (2). These families were well-educated and prepared to teach core subjects, as well as specific content, to their children. (Research indicates that homeschooling families often use tutors and other experts for secondary-level coursework.)

O   What categories of instruction are the most challenging? Seven of the 20 respondents indicated that teaching cultural identity was most challenging, primarily because of the difficulty in finding materials. A few stated that in their geographic area, it was a challenge finding other Black homeschooling families to provide socialization experiences for their children.

O   What strategies do you use to ensure student success? Of the respondents, 50% indicated that individualizing curriculum and instruction or designing a curriculum around the best interests of the child is most important to ensure that child's success. Others noted the importance of teaching moral responsibility, character, behavior, etc., which they believed to be better at than their children's schools.

Remember that homeschooling doesn't just consist of kids sitting around the kitchen table writing in notebooks while mom looks on. There are, of course, government and district regulatory practices that parents must follow. But within those constraints, children can partic ipate in a large variety of activities, from Internet research to field trips to museums and zoos. Sometimes parents in different homeschooling families collaborate to get their children together for special projects or social gatherings. Homeschooling support groups can also help. In addition, some children benefit from being partially homeschooled, in which they learn academic subjects at home, but they attend their local public school to participate in sports and social or leadership activities. Different school districts have different policies on partial homeschooling, though, so parents should do their research before deciding upon a course of action. The point is, however, that there are a variety of options available to make your child's homeschooling experience work for your family.

There Are Choices

Many families just like yours decide to choose the type of educational program that best suits their child's needs. Sometimes public schools are refreshingly accommodating, with teachers and administrators willing to work hard and employ a wide range of options that will ensure that your child is challenged, and his academic and social-emotional needs are met. Unfortunately, this is not the case for many families of gifted children. Public schools often don't have the resources—or even the inclination, in some instances—to provide appropriate educational alternatives for their gifted students. Highly able minority children are at a further disadvantage when they are the only gifted student of their race in their class.

When a gifted child needs more than what the public school system can offer, parents have other options. Private and independent schools and homeschooling are some of them, but there are others. Don't be afraid to search out alternatives—it could be the best thing you do to provide a happy and fulfilling future for your child.

CHAPTER 7

Books, Storytelling, and the Power of Words

Somewhere around six years old, my father read out loud
the words of James Weldon Johnson, Paul Laurence Dunbar,
Gwendolyn Brooks, and Langston Hughes. My father
relished and touted the genius of these writers.

~Charlotte Blake Alston, storyteller

I fondly recall spending long hours in my neighborhood public library and in the library at my elementary school when I was a child. My oldest sister first took me to visit the public library when I was five years old. It was just a few blocks away from our home in Newark, New Jersey. As we entered the halls, I knew we were in a special, magical place. The children's section on the second floor was where we met the librarian, who took me to sections of books that might be of interest to a girl my age. I remember proudly telling the librarian that my sister had already purchased two books for me—*Black Beauty* and *Grimm's Fairy Tales*—and that the books were mine to keep. These books, and others like them, were portals to new and exciting places where I could explore, learn about new ideas and new people, find comfort, and discover things about myself.

In elementary school, I became a library helper. To this day, I remember my first day "on the job." The school librarian, Mr. Foster (not his real name), told me all about the library and explained how the books were organized. I enjoyed the library so much! Of course, I loved the books, but I also relished the solitude, the quiet, and the peace there. The atmosphere felt powerful to me; it was as if all the books with all of their words must have contained everything that anyone would need to know to live a happy and fulfilling life. In the library, I felt a sense of belonging and hopefulness in my spirit that no matter what deficiencies I would face, books would be the great equalizer. I also realized that once I had the words and an understanding of them in my mind, there was nothing anyone could do to erase them.

Other fond memories of my childhood revolve around my family's preoccupation with reading. My mother was always an avid reader. In the evenings after she came home from work, I would sit in her lap as she read to me. She read poetry, introducing me to Langston Hughes, Alfred Lord Tennyson, and Paul Laurence Dunbar. When my father worked the day shift, he and I would get up early in the morning and we would talk and read the newspaper together. He'd tell me what he was reading about and help me understand what was going on in the world around me. Soon, I was able to read the newspaper for myself. Those special times with each of my parents provided me with rich memories and instilled in me the value of reading that has stayed with me for a lifetime.

Reading opened new worlds for me, took me beyond where I was, and allowed me to find comfort and excitement while learning about what I could expect as I grew up. The written word captured me in my early years and never let me go. Though this is my story, I am sure it rings true with gifted children of all ages and from all communities. However, learning to read and understand the printed word is a privilege that Blacks were once denied in this country—a privilege which seems so fundamental and the denial of which seems outrageously discriminatory. Despite a strong oral tradition, Black people understood that the ability to read could provide a foundation for success and freedom, and so they fought for the right to learn to read, and they prevailed. I owe many of my fondest childhood memories to the generations before me who believed that books and reading should be available to everyone.

"Mirror" Books and "Window" Books

Parents like you, as well as school personnel such as librarians, teachers, and principals, know many children who always seem to "have their head in a book." These children find challenge, solace, and excitement in the printed word; they have discovered that books can be a source of comfort and friendship.

Gifted children, particularly if they are in a setting in which they feel alone and isolated from others because of their differentness, may immerse themselves in reading. In books, they can travel to far-away lands, experience different time periods, and read about others who share their interests and goals. Reading books also helps children move independently through different levels of comprehension. Children gain basic understandings of words and word connections as they read, and when they begin reading at higher levels, they not only encounter more intricate sentence structure, diverse elements of language, and complex themes, they also are challenged to analyze and form opinions about what they have read.

As a parent of gifted child, it is very important that you actively support your child's love of reading; visits to the library, trips to bookstores, and reading aloud should be a part of your regular routine. What you do in your home to encourage reading matters more than you might think. Educational researchers have found that reading performance and achievement in school depends more on activities in the home than activities in the school. In addition, Black gifted students who are high achievers frequently report that their parents require reading time in the home.

If you want to encourage your child to read more but don't know where to start, I have compiled a list of current "mirror" books in Appendix II. These are books written for Black children and teens by authors focused on representation in reading materials across genres. You should also go to the diversebooks.org, "We Need Diverse Books" is a non-profit organization dedicated to sharing literature that reflects and honors the lives of all young people. Mirror books are excellent to use with children based on issues they may be facing at various points in their social, emotional and physical development. One such strategy is bibliotherapy. In bibliotherapy, a child reads a book in which the main character deals with issues or concerns similar to those in the child's own life. As the child reads, she can vicariously identify with the character, which will help her to feel less alone in her struggles, since she can see that others have dealt with the same problems that she is facing.

Children get the most out of bibliotherapy when they have an opportunity to discuss the book with a trusted adult who has also read it, whether that adult is a parent, teacher, counselor, or even a therapist. This adult can help the child to make connections between the book and the child's own experiences. Donna Y. Ford, Ph.D., a noted researcher and author whose work has broken new ground in the field of gifted education for Black students, also recommends bibliotherapy to promote self-understanding, racial pride, persistence, and resilience for Black students (Ford, Walters, Byrd & Harris, 2019).

Using books for bibliotherapy can be of immense value to your child, as well as to you, the parent. Discussing characters, ideas, and themes in a book provide an outlet for your child's feelings, even though the discussions may only be about the characters in the book, and not the child. These discussions will also help parents better understand their child and what she is thinking or experiencing. Many of the titles that appear in the appendices of this book are useful resources for this process.

Whether you engage in bibliotherapy with your gifted child or not, you will want to make sure that you choose the right books for him to read. Reading proficiency is linked to a child's ability to "connect" with the reading material, so it is important to select books that are interesting and engaging to your child. Halsted also suggests that you look for books that "stretch" your child's abilities by using challenging vocabulary, complex characters, and interesting plots and settings. However, books that are too difficult may discourage children from reading. When children are appropriately challenged in their reading material, it helps them to become better readers (Schroth., Watson-Thompson, Davis, 2022).

The concept of "mirror" books and "window" books was first introduced by Rudine Sims Bishop, Ed.D., a leading scholar in the field of Black children's literature. She suggested that children be given books that reflect who they are (mirror), as well as books that open worlds larger than the ones they know (window). These kinds of books allow for the continuing development of self-confidence and identity in Black gifted children as they learn about themselves and the world around them.

Appendix II in this book lists several good "mirror" books for Black children, with a variety of selections ranging from biographies to picture books. When you visit schools or public libraries, ask the librarian to tell you of any new books that have been published by Black authors that will help you extend your child's collection of "mirror" books.

Many of the classics are good "window" books. The classics consist of works by authors like Giovanni, L'Engle, Dickens, Dickenson, Wright, Austen, that have stood the test of time by remaining widely read and revered by booklovers everywhere. The themes in most classic books tend to be universal, meaning that they can be appreciated by all children, regardless of race, class, or gender. Gifted students are often intrigued by stories with complex plots, interesting characters, and extensions into "other worlds." Classic books usually contain these elements, and they help children develop their vocabularies, increase their repertoire of literary works, and give them a sense of the possibilities of expression in language. Reading the classics can also help your child's development of historical understandings and critical thinking skills.

Classics that are written by Black authors are also "mirror" books for Black children. Michael C. Thompson, an expert in language arts instruction for gifted children, has compiled a list of authors whose works are considered classics, including several Black writers. These include W.E.B. Du Bois, Frederick Douglass, Booker T. Washington, Toni Morrison, James Baldwin, Lorraine Hansberry, Maya Angelou, Richard Wright, Chinua Achebe, and Ralph Ellison. Other well-known Black authors are Langston Hughes, John Edgar Widemann, Alice Walker, August Wilson, Martin Luther King, Jr., Paul Laurence

Dunbar, Nikki Giovanni, Rita Dove, Sterling Brown, Amiri Baraka, and Mari Evans, Jacquline Woodson, Walter Dean Myers, Maya Angelou, Amanda Gorman, Ta-Nahesi Coates, and Octavia Butler. All of these authors broke new ground in poetry, fiction, non-fiction, science fiction, and theatre. An excellent resource for locating the works of Black authors is the African American Literature Book Club (http://aalbc.com).

As a parent, you should be aware that your gifted child may be capable of reading an advanced-level book but not be emotionally mature or experienced enough to comprehend it. You will need to use your judgment and choose titles for your child that contain material appropriate for his emotional level. You may also need to be prepared to talk with your child about these types of issues.

Black Poets

One of the first published Black writers was Phyllis Wheatley. Born in Senegal, West Africa, in 1753, Phyllis was sold as a slave at an early age to a prosperous family headed by John and Susannah Wheatley. The Wheatleys discovered how gifted Phyllis was and helped her get her poetry published. As a result, her first book of poetry, titled *Poems on Various Subjects*, came out when she was just a teenager (Wideman, 2001).

Paul Laurence Dunbar, the son of former slaves, was born in Dayton, Ohio, in 1892 and later became known as the Father of Black Poetry. What was remarkable about Dunbar's poetry was that he wrote and published in both the dialect of the Black people of his day as well as in the more formal English tradition. A very gifted writer, Dunbar's first collection of poetry, titled *Lyrics of Lowly Life*, was published when he was just 24 years old (Braxton, 1993).

Like Phyllis Wheatley, who was said to have written her first poem at age six, Dunbar also wrote his first poem at age six, and he gave his first public recital at age nine. He was a very prolific writer from the time he was a young student. Early in his life, many of

---

his poems appeared in some of the most popular and widely read journals of his time, including *Harper's Weekly* and the *Saturday Evening Post*. Today, literary scholars view Dunbar's career as having transcended race and locale, enabling him to be the first Black writer whose work was recognized and well-respected within both the Black and White communities.

The Oral Tradition of Debating

Because Blacks were denied the right to learn to read when they were first introduced to American soil, they have an unusually strong oral tradition in this country. Blacks have been known for using their keen verbal skills to convince, cajole, and encourage their people.

Historically, early schools for Black children included oratory within the curriculum, though now it is rare. During oratory sessions in class, students practiced speaking aloud to an audience. The speaking assignments may have been as simple as reciting a poem or as complicated as memorizing and delivering a political speech, such as the Gettysburg Address or a speech by Frederick Douglass or another noted Black leader. The tradition of storytelling has been passed down for generations from the oral traditions of the African continent. Storytelling was a way of preserving and passing down values, history, codes, norms. As an enslaved people in America, Africans maintained this cultural legacy over the generations (Utley, 2008).

It seems clear, then, why Black students have excelled at debate and oratory. For a vivid historical perspective on this topic, both parents and their children will enjoy the 2007 movie *The Great Debaters* (starring and directed by Denzel Washington and produced by Oprah Winfrey), which illustrates the true story of the Wiley College debate team of Marshall, Texas. Wiley was the first historically Black college to compete and win a debate contest against the University of Southern California (portrayed in the movie as Harvard College), who at the time was the reigning champion. The story focuses on the determination and inspiration of Wiley's debate team leader, Melvin B. Tolson,

English professor and poet, as well as the wit and conviction of the young debaters. After their initial victory, Wiley's debate team went undefeated for 10 years, from 1935 to 1945 (Hailey, 2007).

The debaters in the film are based on real individuals, and in one case, a composite of several characters. One character was James Farmer, Jr., who later helped establish the Southern Christian Leadership Conference, one of the nation's earliest civil rights organizations. Samantha Brooke, the only female member of the team, is based on the character of Henrietta Bell, who later became a social worker.

For teachers, parents, and community leaders interested in organizing and operating debate teams today, *The Great Debaters* is an excellent tool. Throughout the movie, viewers see the life-wrenching challenges that the debaters and their leader faced as racism and discrimination plagued the Southern towns they visited. While the story has an underlying theme of the civil rights efforts led by Professor Tolson, it also provides visual and verbal examples of the type of preparation needed for Black students to become award-winning debaters, as well as portrayals of the actual debates in which the students participated.

Debate and other oral presentation competitions are types of forensic activities. Many schools have forensic teams. If your child appears to have a gift for speaking, convincing others of her viewpoint, and articulating well in the presence of an audience, then joining a forensics team can be a great way for her to develop her strengths. Often, gifted learners who are more introverted and less likely to socialize will find forensics competitions to be an excellent outlet for expressing their strong opinions and ideas about subjects of interest and importance.

Young people who are able to prepare a written argument to support a cause have the potential and the skills to be successful in a variety of fields, including law, education, business, and politics. A recent and notable example is President Barack Obama. Even those who dislike him must admit that he is a skilled orator. Based on speeches he has given around the world, President Obama is destined to go down in history as one of our country's great speechmakers.

If your gifted learner has an inclination toward speechmaking, you can support him by exposing him to great speeches and speechmakers. You may want to give him the book *Great Speeches of African Americans,* which contains speeches by men and women marking significant periods of change in our country, including slavery, abolitionism, reconstruction, and civil rights. In addition, encourage your child to participate in any public speaking opportunities at school and in church, as well as in speechmaking contests.

Speechmaking that Helped Change History
One memorable speech from our country's history is that of a fugitive slave speaking at a City Hall meeting in Syracuse, New York, concerning the Fugitive Slave Act of 1850. The slave, Jermain Wesley Loguen, was so convincing that the citizens of Syracuse later voted to declare their town a refuge for freed slaves.

Storytelling: An Ancient Art Revived

Storytellers are performers who use their memory and their passion for the spoken word to appeal to others. The tradition of storytelling began in the villages of Africa many generations ago with the village *griot* (pronounced *gri-ou*), who was a poet and praise singer. This griot was known for his large storehouse of information, which he recalled from memory and used to entertain and inform his audiences. When Africans came to America, they brought with them the tradition of imparting information through these types of oral methods—i.e., storytelling. This ancient tradition within the Black culture has seen a great revival in the past 25 years. Today, virtually everyone in the Black community knows a neighbor or family member who serves as a historian for the family or community through the art of storytelling.

Good storytellers have the ability to hold the attention of their listeners through their use of colorful and interesting language, vivid expressions, and animated body movements. Listening to a storyteller recall memories of special events and meaningful exchanges from the family or community enriches us. Their stories connect us to the past and can teach important lessons to our gifted child for the future.

Often, storytellers are genius tale weavers who display their talents young. As such, many are discovered in childhood and nurtured within the community. If your gifted child enjoys entertaining and capturing the interest of others with his stories and dramatic interpretations, the art of storytelling holds great promise as an outlet for his gifts and talents. Storytelling festivals are hosted through arts agencies, museums, foundations, and storytelling associations across the country each year; attending a storytelling festival can be a culturally enriching experience for the entire family. As a parent of a gifted child, you may also be interested in bringing storytelling to your own neighborhood by hosting a program in your community center, church, or school, extending this valuable tradition throughout your community.

Rap Music: A Contemporary American Phenomenon

In addition to the oral tradition of storytelling, the vocal style of the African griots also led to the rise of the musical genre which we call "rap." Much like the blues and jazz of the last century, rap music as an art form was a natural progression for Black youth. The culture of rap music began in the United States as an outgrowth of the Civil Rights Movement and the desire for Black artists to voice their feelings and speak for their whole communities. Rap is a complex combination of speechmaking, storytelling, political discussion, poetry, and the spoken word—all converging in an underlying foundation of music.

Rap music and the growth of the "hip hop" generation has provided a voice for urban America, in particular those suffering under the vestiges of poverty, crime, poor educational systems, and violence in their neighborhoods, and the young artists who struggle to bring their messages to the public in this way are sometimes very gifted individuals. One of rap music's greatest artists, Tupac Shakur, began writing poetry as a young man living in an impoverished urban community. Shakur's early poetry, written when he was just 19 years old, is deeply expressive and moving, reflecting the mind and spirit of an exceptionally gifted young man. His first collection of poetry was published in 1999, three years after his death at age 25 (Shakur, 1999).

Shakur's ability to create poetry was undoubtedly linked with his ability to create music with strong rhythm and rhyme schemes. His experience is not unique. Unfortunately, there is great controversy surrounding rap music. Some very popular hip hop artists produce songs with lyrics that promote sexuality, drugs, and violence, and many people are concerned about the influence that these messages have on their children. Young people today will very likely be exposed to this type of rap music, and as a parent of a Black gifted child or teenager, it is important that you discuss the influence of the hip-hop culture on your child's life. To attempt to shelter children completely from rap music is probably futile—what began as an art form primarily heard in Black communities has now reached far across racial, cultural, and class boundaries.

How do you as a parent enable your children to learn about the positive influences of rap music, rap artists, and the legacy of Black America from which the music originates? How can you help them deal honestly with the negative influences of this multi-million-dollar art form turned music industry? As with other difficult or complex topics, family conversations are often the most effective way parents have to influence their children's decision making and school achievement. Bring discussions about rap music and its potential conflicts with your family's values to the family dinner table. However, before you begin conversations that are negative or judgmental about musical forms today and their influence on children, remind yourself of how your parents initially responded to music and cultural influences when you were a teenager. Remembering those early experiences— during which your parents may have been very critical, which likely only made you want to rebel—may help you to have smoother, more open conversations with your own children.

When children have early experiences with positive values and understand the devastating effects of discriminatory music, books, films, and political speeches, they learn to make good decisions based on facts as well as their own interests. In your conversations, provide positive information about rap music as an art form, and discuss how its influences have changed the culture of America. Many hip hop and rap artists are multi-talented young men and women who contribute portions of their profits to their home communities. Some have started educational foundations, donated funds to health and welfare organizations, and taken the lead in campaigning for relief for citizens after natural disasters. Others have left music to become business leaders, actors, fashion icons, and even politicians. These artists often share a message of social justice that speaks to the youth culture.

If you have instilled core values in your children, then your gifted teens, with their intense sensitivities and higher cognitive understandings, will know what's positive and beneficial to society and what is not, and they will choose their music accordingly. As a parent of teens today, sharing your children's interests will mean helping them make good choices, and you can only do that by understanding the underlying messages of their music and then dis cussing the positives and negatives. Keeping an open mind and communicating openly and honestly will show respect for your children's viewpoints. It will also make your gifted adolescents more likely to respect your opinion and be more inclined to listen to and heed your advice.

Nurturing a Love of Words in Our Children

We know from research that children who have a variety of experiences with language have an advantage in school. Nearly every subject and discipline relies on language as a way to communicate it, so even if your child strives to become a research scientist or an art historian, she'll need to master language in order to get there. You can find many enrichment opportunities to encourage your child's interest in and passion for reading, writing, and speaking. Some of your greatest resources may be as close as your own family, your child's school, your public library, or even your church. For example, many libraries and bookstores offer story hours and other reading-related activities for children. You may also want to partner with other parents to share literary arts opportunities across your community.

Despite the technological advances in our culture today, one of the best ways to enhance your children's appreciation for and mastery of language is to encourage them to read, read, and read. Reading opens up new ideas and concepts, helps people understand the world in a more complete way, and gives children opportunities to discover their heritage. In addition, being knowledgeable about many things—or even just one thing—can increase a child's self-confidence and self-esteem.

As a parent, you want to empower your child. Information from books and other resources become your child's arsenal of knowledge. When your child reads, the information gleaned from the printed source— be it a book, newspaper, or magazine article—becomes knowledge that is his forever. Once it is captured, no one can ever take it away.

Parents can use the following activities to encourage and nurture a love in their children for the written and spoken word:

○ *Encourage your child to write in a journal or notebook:* In addition to reading, children also develop their language skills by writing. Encourage your gifted child to keep a journal for daily reflections and self-examinations. Children can also use journals and notebooks as a place to jot down drafts of poems or stories they may be thinking of. Tupac Shakur's poetry book, noted earlier, was published from his own hand-written notes in his journals. Give your child blank journals and notebooks, along with a safe place to keep them. Alternatively, some children may want to keep their journals electronically, using a computer to type their words instead of writing them. This is okay. The important thing is that they're putting their thoughts and ideas into words.

○ *Create a personal bookshelf:* A bookshelf that belongs exclusively to the child for her books and journals alone can be a terrific way to support her reading and writing. If possible, inscribe the child's name on the bookshelf. Also, allow your child to decide where to place the bookshelf in her room or in the house so that she can access it when she feels the urge to read or write.

○ *Build reading time into the family schedule:* A regular, consistent time built into the family schedule for reading—whether the family reads books together or independently—helps children see the value of reading, as it is given a priority over other tasks at least some of the time in the family's schedule. Reading time for all allows parents to model reading to their children, and when everyone is reading the same book, it can stimulate interesting discussions.

○ *Establish a book club:* In traditional book clubs, a book is selected that everyone will read and discuss at a chosen time. This gives children opportunities to talk about what they have read and share their opinions with others. To assist with the costs of purchasing the books for the members of the club, you could have children conduct a fundraiser and then, later, sell the books through Amazon.com or at a yard sale. Children might also consider giving the books to a children's home, school, church, or other charity.

○ *Trade books with others in your community or church:* Book trading allows children to share their books with others. Book trading clubs can be generated within the community or even among a small group of friends and are a wonderful way for children to find others with similar interests. An added benefit is that children may end up reading books that they would not normally choose themselves, which may lead them to new and exciting topics of interest.

○ *Use education material to teach literary analysis:* As a parent, you may be interested in accessing materials that are published for educators and generally only used in schools to teach literary analysis. One highly recommended resource is Navigators, developed by staff at the Center for Gifted Education at The College of William and Mary in Virginia. The Navigator guide can be used with specified books or as a guide for interpreting and analyzing similar books. The Great Books series is another resource used by many schools to teach critical thinking and literary analysis to small groups of children, usually in gifted or advanced learner programs. Ask your child's teacher if Navigators or the Great Books series have been considered as resources for their school's English/language arts department. You could even volunteer to serve as a Great Books leader.

○ *Study famous speeches by Black orators:* For children who are interested in sharpening their speechmaking skills, reading copies of famous speeches can be of great assistance. Children can study speeches by Black orators like Martin Luther King, Jr., Sojourner Truth, Frederick Douglass, Ida B. Wells-Barnett, Mary McCleod Bethune, Barbara Jordan, President Barack Obama and Amanda Gorman (Daley, 2006). For extra challenge, a child can study a selected speech and host a speech recital at your home, in the church, or in a community setting. If this goes well and the child is excited to continue challenging himself at even higher levels, you may be able to have his teacher set up a speech recital in the school for all students. You might also sponsor a speechmaking contest within your church or community center. Provide topics and examples of famous speeches, set guidelines, offer awards, establish a panel of judges (peer or adult), set the date for the competition, advertise, and have a great time!

○ *Organize forensics clubs:* If your adolescent is deeply passionate about moral, social, and political affairs, encourage her to participate in forensics. Speak with her teachers to find out if the school sponsors a forensics club or has a debate team. If not, volunteer to assist in organizing one at your school, at a community center, or in your church. Host a training session with a debate teacher to provide guidance.

○ *Engage in storytelling:* Attend storytelling events in community libraries, churches, and at festivals. Encourage your child to create an account of your family's history that can be shared through storytelling at the next family gathering. You can also ask that an elder in the family tell special stories at the next gathering so that children can see how stories change with time and perspective.

○ *Write poetry:* Encourage your child to write poetry. If your child discovers an affinity for it, you can encourage him to publish some of his poems at www.poetry.com. Children interested in poetry can also create a book of family poetry or develop a biography of a poet that they enjoy reading. A few excellent resources for promising young poets are:

- Potato Hill Poetry: www.potatohill.com
- Meryln's Pen: www.merlynspen.com
- Lift Every Voice: www.africanamericanpoetry.org
- Stone Soup: www.stonesoup.com
- Anthology of Poetry, Inc.,
  148 Sunset Ave., P.O. Box 698, Asheboro, NC 27204

○ *Develop read-aloud books for other children:* Gifted children often enjoy helping younger children learn reading skills and setting up opportunities for them to read to younger students can be mutually rewarding. Budding writers also can write their own books and share them with others. This will help increase their understanding of how to write for different audiences, and the feedback they get can be invaluable.

Those who like to draw or paint might also choose to illustrate their books. When creating a read-aloud book for elementary- or middle school-age children, there are seven guidelines to follow (Baytops, 2009):

- Consider the audience's age, interests, and vocabulary.
- Design the book to teach a moral or lesson.
- Carefully select which part of the text will be illustrated.
- Use simple sentence structure and basic words, or write the book in poetic verse.
- Keep the storyline simple; ensure that the character has only one issue or problem to deal with.
- Make sure the characters' actions fit within the theme of the story.

Write, illustrate, and review the book. Parents, you can edit the text as necessary, but remember that the story and illustrations belong to the author.

The greatest gift we can give our children is the ability to achieve their goals and succeed in life, and whatever their ambitions, they will likely need a solid education to get there. Not all children like to read, but if we as parents can instill in them an understanding of the value of the written word, perhaps even those children who are reluctant to pick up a book will ultimately find enjoyment in reading, writing, and oral activities such as speechmaking, debating, and storytelling. Creative outlets such as these will encourage children's critical thinking skills and give them yet another avenue that can lead to success.

CHAPTER 8

Teaching Your Child to Survive and Thrive

Success is the process of learning and growing. It requires that the individual step out of line, away from the pack, and march to the beat of a different, sometimes distant, drummer.

~Dennis Kimbro, motivational speaker and author

Every day, our children are bombarded with messages about what it means to be successful in contemporary society. The media usually displays success from a financial viewpoint, showing off the lives of wealthy, high-profile athletes, musicians, actors, and politicians. These people live in enormous houses, drive expensive cars, and only wear the latest fashions. Legitimately, many of these individuals have worked hard to accomplish their level of fame and achievement, and some of them regularly share their financial success with others through foundations, special schools, and other programs that they have developed.

Monetary wealth, however, is not necessarily the only definition of success that we want our children to learn. Certainly, there is a satisfaction that comes from being able to have nice things, but there are other meanings of success that are perhaps more important. Dennis Kimbro, Ph.D., motivational speaker and author, defines success as follows:

○ Success is knowing yourself and what you want.

○ Success is born by the pursuit of a goal or an ideal which will benefit others as easily as the dreamer.

○ Success cannot be conferred upon others.

○ Success can only be earned through individual initiative.

○ Succeeding means risk taking, courage, faith, and commitment. Frederick Douglass was correct: success is born of struggle.

○ Success demands the use of whatever abilities and talents are available.

○ The achiever will be most successful doing what he or she truly enjoys.

As a parent, you must help your child define success in ways that will be socially, emotionally, spiritually, and intellectually beneficial to him. You want to challenge your child to develop a "success mentality" that will enable him to make the most of the experiences that he has as he works toward a successful life in a career that holds meaning for him, as well as one that allows him to use his exceptional abilities for the benefit of others. Fortunately, gifted children have a strong ability to see success on a broader scale—how it can be attained in many different ways and then used to contribute to the greater good.

Talk to your child about her unique strengths and how focusing on those strengths can assist in the development of her plans for the future. You can also help your child develop a broader framework for success by exposing her to stories of individuals who are like her, who have the same kinds of interests, and who have been successful across many different fields. There are numerous biographies available describing Blacks who have been able to make a difference in their communities, the nation, and the world at large. Some of these men and women courageously entered careers that were traditionally not open to Blacks. Others rose to the top of their field and influenced the lives of many with their great discoveries, published writings, artwork displays, and music recordings. Children will be inspired by reading about the lives of these individuals.

The Academy of Achievement in Washington, DC, was established in 1961 as a living museum to profile achievers across the fields of business, sports, public service, science, and the arts from around the world. It identified seven keys to success: *passion, vision, preparation, courage, perseverance, integrity,* and the *American dream.* On its website www.academyofachievement.com, honorees provide insights into how these characteristics have influenced the course of their lives. Honorees include Simone Biles (Olympic gymnast); Oprah Winfrey (business-woman, entertainer, and philanthropist), Maya Angelou (poet and activist), and Benjamin Carson, Ph.D., (pediatric neurosurgeon from Johns Hopkins University); Bill Russell (basketball player and civil rights activist), Coretta Scott King (civil rights activist) and Desmond Tutu (theologian and social justice activist). Even though their histories and circumstances, as well as their accolades and successes, are very different from one another, these honorees recount stories with similar themes of survival, resiliency, and sheer strength of spirit. Like others, these Black honorees have achieved success because they were hard working, courageous, and dedicated to achieving their dreams.

As a parent of a gifted student, you will witness your child moving through many different life stages and events which will challenge him in one way or another. Whether your child will emerge from these experiences successfully will depend not only on how he responds to them, but also on the type of support he has from family and friends.

Navigating through Multiple Worlds

Sometimes gifted minorities do what others may call "sacrificing their race," becoming more like the dominant race in order to succeed. Some Blacks (and other minorities) who want to succeed in a predom-inately White society feel that they must learn how to "talk White," "act White," and use White social customs rather than their own. There are plenty of biographical accounts, dating back well over a century, of successful Blacks who have struggled with the challenge of "living between two races."

In 1903, W.E.B. Du Bois wrote about his struggles as a gifted Black man functioning in a predominantly White American society. Du Bois attended an all-White high school and, later, a graduate school at a highly selective university where the vast majority of the students were White. In his book *The Souls of Black Folks*, he describes the psychological pain of what he called the "two warring ideals (DuBois, 1903):

> *One ever feels his two-ness,—an American, a Negro; two souls, two thoughts, two unreconciled strivings; two warring ideals in one dark body, whose dogged strength alone keeps it from being torn asunder.*

Many Black gifted students report similar feelings today when they participate in gifted programs in which they are a minority—sometimes so much so that they are the only Black student identified as gifted within their class. The notion of "acting White" to succeed in their academic and intellectual endeavors is difficult for some high-achieving Black students to swallow, and they may underachieve to avoid these kinds of accusations from their peers. It is important to note, however, that many Black gifted students enjoy success in their gifted programs, despite allegations that they are "turning their back on their race," and despite being only one of a few Blacks in the class.

"Acting White" is a concept that derogatorily refers to Blacks who use proper English when speaking, dress in a way that is different from what is currently popular in the Black culture, do well in school and attain high grades, and demonstrate other characteristics that some people attribute solely to academically oriented White students. In a revealing study, Signithia Fordham, Ph.D. and Dr. John Ogbu, Ph.D., found that Black students who were given high-level coursework or placed in programs for bright students expressed fear of harassment for "not being Black enough" from others in their communities, especially from other students their age.

Although these kinds of negative stereotypes are sometimes associated with Black students who perform well in school, not all high-achieving Black students dislike being "the smart one." Some take pride in their academic achievements, describing how schoolmates and community members admire them and support them in their intellectual and academic efforts (Stinson, 2010).

One case study that illustrates this point well is John, a Black student who was accepted into one of Virginia's Governor's Schools, a specialized advanced program for gifted and talented students. Virginia has academic-year, summer residential, and summer regional Governor's Schools programs operating across the state. The program that John attended was a half-day program where he was allowed to take advanced math, science, and technology coursework that was not offered at his small rural high school. In addition to attending the Governor's School, John graduated valedictorian of his class and was accepted at four universities. He chose the University of Virginia and is currently pursuing a degree in architecture.

In an interview, John's mother described how and why her son was able to maintain his focus on being a high-achieving student, taking full advantage of every opportunity to excel and reach his goals:

Interviewer: How would you describe John's academic experiences in high school, particularly since he was the only Black male or one of the few Black males in his classes? Were his experiences positive, negative, or neither?

Mother: John's experience was very, very positive. He is well known by everyone in the community. At the Governor's School, they accepted him well. I think it had a lot to do with his mannerisms, the way he acted. He always speaks using correct grammar and correct English. I think because of this, his White counterparts accepted him... Some of the Blacks at his school may not have always appreciated the fact that John spoke and behaved as he did, but he always treated everyone with the same respect. His teachers at the Governor's School liked him a lot..., offering him tutoring to help him through his courses. The other students from his school who attended dropped out of the program early; John stuck it out. John doesn't go out of his way to try to fit in with his Black peers. I know that when he goes to college, he'll find more Black students just like him—bright and determined to be successful—but in high school, it wasn't always like that. So many times his social peers were White students in the special program, but it didn't matter to John. He was always the same no matter who he was around, and I think people expected that of him and respected him for it.

Who have been members of his circle of support?

Our family—his father, brother, and myself. At church we try to encourage the youth; the pastor is always encouraging them and speaking about their future. [John's] principal and guidance counselor at his high school and the teachers at the Governor's School were excellent.

Have there been any conflicts in the family or neighborhood because of John's school success? If so, how did you handle it?

Nothing open—maybe more subtle. I-G-N-O-R-E! [spelled out] is what I've told my sons. You belong to God, given to us to raise. You have got to show God to the world by showing the God in you. God don't want you messing up.

What strengths does John have that will enable him to be a successful college student?

Work ethic, determination…the power of prayer, faith. I always remind my sons, "Don't forget to pray. God is always there." John understands this. He'll miss our family conversations. We talk about everything at the dinner table—important things like education, health, sexual promiscuity. We try our best to…listen and answer. At the end of the conversation, their dad asks, "Do you have any more questions?" [John] will miss that, but he knows that he can call us and tell us anything, and we'll do all we can to help him. Our support will remain the same. The school he chose is very large and competitive, but I think that John will take advantage of programming on campus that he needs and that he'll do just fine, even on the large campus. He'll do just fine.

What a wonderful exchange! This young Black man was not only intellectually gifted, he also had the gift of a warm and supportive family, who nurtured his success through open family conversations and messages of strength against adversity.

Today, programs operating across the country offer challenging academic experiences for Black and other minority students. In addition, an increasing number of high schools are focusing attention on providing Black students with advanced coursework and opportunities for college preparation. Making AP courses, honors courses, and other advanced programming more available to Black students enables schools to raise their overall achievement. In the end, everyone benefits—students, schools, school districts, communities, and society at large. However, one of the most significant advantages of this nationwide effort to support academic success in our young Blacks is that we are finding more and more Black students who enjoy scholarly activities and are proud of their achievements.

This is not to say that these students still don't struggle with the stigma of "acting White" or the isolation that they sometimes feel as a minority in a sea of majority-race students. To address the challenge of coping with a bi-cultural existence—in other words, being a minority in special programs for gifted students—teachers, counselors, and parents must teach and encourage students to maintain a sense of individualism and to be the best of who they are in all set tings. This, of course, is easier said than done. One strategy is to create learning community discussion groups, in which students are given an opportunity to openly talk about the highs and lows of being a cultural minority in gifted and advanced learner programs. Such discussions can provide students with a healthy outlet for their feelings, as well as opportunities to share individual coping strategies. It is recommended that parents, teachers, and counselors work collaboratively to coordinate and supervise these types of meetings. Sometimes students engage in what is known as "code switching," in which they change their behaviors to adapt to different environments. Adjusting behavior, dress, and even language to different situations takes skill and confidence. However, fitting our behavior to the setting is something that most of us do on a daily basis. Our language and dress on the job or while at church, which may be quite formal, is typically very different from the informal behaviors that we engage in at home. When children or adolescents change their behaviors to fit in with different peer groups, they are showing some of these same patterns of adaptability, which are quite normal and acceptable. Just make sure your child knows that she must be true to herself at all times. She may choose to display different aspects of her personality at various times to various people, but her alternating actions and speech are all still facets of her authentic self.

As a parent of a Black child, you should be realistic and honest about who we are in America, even today. Black male college graduates are underemployed at almost twice the rate of their White peers. So even after having obtained a degree, your Black child may suffer from discrimination based solely on his race and not on his qualifications. Some Black male graduates have had to remove any connection to Black fraternal organizations from their resume, and others graduating from Morehouse, Yale, and other prestigious institutions find that they have to change their "ethnic-sounding" name or be concerned about the sound of their voice on the phone in order to effectively compete for jobs. While they may seem archaic, these challenges are very real for Blacks who may be the first with a degree in a career category or the first of their gender to enter a particular field of study.

Your child will undoubtedly be faced with tough choices as she grows and matures—because she is a minority, because she is gifted, and simply because that's a natural part of growing up. As a parent, you must help your child understand that sometimes she will be accepted for who she is and other times she will not—and that's just the way life is. With support from you, your child can learn to maintain her sense of self and confidently express her true nature without being concerned about whether others accept her.

Bearing the Burden and the Blessings of the Race

Many Blacks live with the understanding that they, as individuals, represent their entire race to the majority culture. When a Black person fails at something, the perception often is that all Black people have failed in some way. When a Black person succeeds or even becomes eminent, all Black people are raised up in the wake of this success. This phenomenon is known as "the burden of the race."

Gifted, high-potential, and successful Blacks of all ages are particularly likely to feel that they carry with them the future of all Black people. What a heavy weight for our youth! This burden has another side, though, for when our children experience success, it becomes the success of others like them. In this way, they lift up their entire race, and perhaps their accomplishments will help the world change its negative opinions of Blacks. When this happens, that burden becomes a blessing.

Being the first person to do something is significant. When someone is the first at anything—for example, the first Black man to become President of the United States (President Barack Obama), the first Black woman to become secretary of state (Condoleezza Rice) or Kamala Harris, the first Black woman to become Vice President of the United States or Ketanji Brown Jackson, the first Black woman to become a Supreme Court Justice—their names are remembered, and they become proud representatives of their race. They carry the burden of the race with dignity and honor, uplifting Blacks everywhere. Although the examples used here are of political figures, other eminent Black individuals abound in our culture representing many other areas and disciplines.

One excellent resource for locating "firsts" in the area of mathematics is the Mathematicians of the African Diaspora website (www.math. buffalo.edu/mad), maintained by Scott W. Williams, Ph.D., professor of mathematics at the State University of New York at Buffalo. Williams has created a chronology of Africans and African Americans who have become the first to earn doctoral degrees in mathematics since the late 1800s. The website also provides information on Black physicists, scientists, and computer scientists, as well as support for students working on science projects.

Other resources go back even farther. Recently, scholars have written extensively about the African origins of math and science. These historical accounts include details about the people of Kemet, also known as Egypt, who were the first scientists in Africa. Kemet is known by scholars around the world as the birthplace of geometry. After all, it was the Egyptians who built the Great Pyramids, the design and structure of which have been studied by scientists and historians for centuries. Using the resources found in these websites and others can vastly broaden your gifted child's understanding of the origins of success. This kind of information is invaluable in establishing a foundation of scholarship for young, gifted boys and girls that extends beyond the United States to the shores of Africa. They can only benefit from knowing about Blacks whose roles in the origins of great theories, inventions, and ideas provide the basis for the fields of mathematics, engineering, and science as we know them today. More recent stories of scientists like Benjamin Banneker, George Washington Carver, and Mae Jamison will help your gifted child develop an interest in and excitement for mathematics, technology, engineering, and science.

It is critical to the growth and development of your gifted child that she know that the history of Blacks did not begin with slavery, but as people of the continent of Africa many, many years ago. Her heritage may include slavery and oppression, but she is also a descendent of noble African tribes who changed the world with their ability to discover answers to some of the great mysteries of the universe. Once Africans came to America, their path in history took an abrupt turn, but they once again rose to the challenges of their race. Rather than let your gifted child feel the burden of the race, make her aware of her ability to carry on the blessings of the race, based not only on her sharp intellect and the support that you give her, but also on the foundation of a race of people who were able to do great things.

The Challenge of Finding True Peers

Gifted Black children aren't the only ones who face peer pressure and accusations of turning their backs on their race. As a parent of a gifted learner, you may also be challenged by neighbors and family members who accuse you of trying to separate your child from his traditions and from his own people. If you advocate for appropriately advanced learning opportunities for him, others may contend that you are setting the child up to be arrogant, self-righteous, or conceited. This can be as difficult to bear for adults as the teasing and taunting is for children, but remember, your primary purpose—the most important thing you can do—is to ensure that your child has opportunities to reach his full potential.

Whatever you do, never sacrifice your child's future just to keep peace within the family or neighborhood. Teach your child that if she has to pretend not to be gifted to keep certain friends, then she doesn't need those people as her friends. If they really know her, they will respect and appreciate the fact that she has opportunities to enrich her life and prepare for a successful future through the courses and experiences that are provided for her in the gifted education program and elsewhere.

As a parent, your role is to create a positive, supportive experience in the home setting and to view the school experience as providing a foundation for positive returns when your gifted learner becomes a contributing member of society as an adult. It is important to recognize that your child's school experiences may be very different from his home and community experiences. This is especially the case if your child is one of a very few Black gifted students within a larger group of White children who may come from different neighborhoods. When children of diverse environments participate in the same school programs together, those who are in the minority may not have anyone to talk to or share with who truly understands them. This makes for a very lonely experience.

How do you as a parent address this situation? First, talk to your child. Find out how she feels about being in the gifted program. Listen carefully to what she has to say. In some cases, a child may be so excited and relieved to finally be in an intellectually stimulating environment that she may not pay much attention to "being the only one." As time goes on and she gets to know the other students in the group, she may discover that intellectually, she is finally among peers, and yet in terms of personal experiences, she is still very much alone. Conversely, her intellectual and academic strengths may be the common ground that allows her to find good friends among her

White classmates, and if they become comfortable with one another, she may find that she is able to discuss with these peers how it feels to be a minority in the class. This kind of discussion can be enlightening to majority-race students, who often have never had to contemplate this kind of racial isolation. However, gifted children are frequently empathetic, and they usually know what it feels like to be "the odd man out." Once they recognize how others are feeling, typically they are quick to help alleviate negative situations. An excellent resource for your gifted teen is the updated *Gifted Teens Survival Guide: Smart, Sharp and Ready for Almost Anything* (Galbraith & Delisle, 2022).

Even if your child bonds well with intellectual peers of a different race, he can still greatly benefit, both socially and emotionally, from being with others who are like him. Parents can advocate for other Black children who may be gifted or have high ability but who have been overlooked by the school. Research indicates that students who come into gifted programs with others of similar gender and race stand a better chance of remaining in these programs over time. Creating these types of "cohorts," or groups of similar students, can be one of the most effective ways of addressing your child's discomfort with being in a group of majority-culture gifted learners. When he sees that there are others students in the program who look like him, his comfort level will increase, and he will be more apt to "be himself" and not feel the need to pretend to be like the other students.

Parents can also work with school personnel or community leaders to develop a set of inspirational workshops or mentoring programs for their gifted children, during which adults of similar backgrounds and those from the neighborhood who have become successful in a variety of fields can serve as guest speakers and/or mentors. By sharing their own stories, these types of leaders can encourage gifted children to maintain a strong sense of self.

Accepting Your Children's Other-Race Peers

Being a minority does not mean that all your child's experiences with majority-race children will be negative. As a matter of fact, many children form lifelong friendships with others outside of their race. If your child is in a gifted program that contains predominantly White classmates, she will likely spend a great deal of her time with students who do not look like her. As such, young people of other cultural groups will become not only her intellectual peers, but her social peers as well. These children will develop bonds based on their common interests, common concerns, and common needs for friendship and companionship. Over time, your child will almost certainly become comfortable with other cultural and racial groups, and if she has a solid foundation of self-confidence and self-worth, she will easily maintain her sense of self within any group of individuals. Oftentimes, however, Black children in predominantly White schools suffer from a lack of 'belonging' and not having peers with similar experiences. In these settings, it is very important to talk with your child often and openly ask questions about their school experiences and level of comfort in such environments. One story that has resonated with educators across the nation can be found in Chapter 1 of *Empowering Underrepresented Gifted Students: Perspectives from the field* (Davis & Douglas, 2021). In Chapter 1, students who attended the Pinevew School in Sarasota Florida discuss how they feel as culturally diverse learners in a predominately White school for the gifted. One story is told by a Black female who experienced a lack of belonging that she believes impacted her self-esteem (Konoru, 2021).

As a parent of a minority gifted child, you must keep an open mind to the kinds of friends with which your child finds kinship. Be proud of your child for looking past superficial traits, and accept his racially transcendent behavior as that of a mature individual who has formed bonds with others based on common interests and character—not just on the color of their skin or the texture of their hair. But help your children be aware of discriminating behaviors expressed by others from the same "other" communities and be ready for conversations that may be difficult, yet important regarding racism, inequities, and social justice issues that all Black students and their families face on a regular basis.

Positive Peer Relationships

Drs. Sampson Davis, George Jenkins, and Rameck Hunt, are fondly known as the "Three Doctors." As teenage boys growing up on the tough inner-city streets of Newark, New Jersey, these three kindred spirits made a pact: they would stick together to go to college, graduate, and become doctors. Now, several years later, these three men have overcome countless obstacles and proudly serve as the face of health and education for youth and families across the country.

Today, Dr. Davis is a board-certified Emergency Medicine Physician at St. Michael's Medical Center and Raritan Bay Medical Center. Dr. Jenkins serves as Assistant Professor of Clinical Dentistry at Columbia University. Dr. Hunt is a board- certified internist at University Medical Center at Princeton and Assistant Professor of Medicine at Robert Wood Johnson Medical School. Additionally, these three doctors have authored three inspiring books about their lives: The Pact, for adults, We Beat the Streets, for children, and The Bond, which highlights fatherhood relationships.

Growing up in the streets of Newark, these men know firsthand the pressures and struggles of life in the inner city and how difficult it can be going at it alone. Determined not to become victims of their environment, the trio stood firm in their mission and together became a remarkable success story of inspiration, dedication, and determination. Their book The Pact is used at high schools, colleges, and universities nationwide. In addition, these men are some of the most sought-after motivational speakers in the country, together symbolizing how perseverance, resiliency, and commitment to their goals helped them succeed.

The Power of Positive Support

Whether your gifted child finds friends from within her own culture or outside of it, she will rely on these friendships to support her as she navigates through life's twists and turns. An excellent example of the kind of camaraderie that can motivate and sustain our gifted children as they strive to succeed is the true story of three gifted young Black men who grew up in the inner city of Newark, New Jersey. Although they were surrounded by negative influences and had few positive role models, they each went on to earn doctoral degrees and become very successful in their field (Davis, Jenkins, Hunt & Page, 2003). Their story is particularly interesting because these three young men made a promise to help each other accomplish their goals, and they did so by supporting each other throughout high school, college, and medical school. In their book *The Pact: Three Young Men Make a Promise and Fulfill a Dream*, which became a *New York Times* Best Seller, they write: "We found in one another a friendship that works in a powerful way…that helped three vulnerable boys grow into successful men…a friendship that ultimately helped save our lives" (Sampson, et. al., 2003).

As a parent, you may find that others in the community, such as neighbors or family friends, feel a sense of responsibility to help nurture your child. The more people who wish to help your child succeed, the better! Gifted children and teens can sometimes find support in unusual places and through interesting individuals. Positive role models are not necessarily famous or eminent people. Our gifted youth have an affinity for locating the people who will help lift them up and achieve their dreams.

As an example, consider the movie *Lackawanna Blues*. This is the story of a young Black boy, Ruben, who grows up in a neighbor's boarding house in Lackawanna, New York, because his mother is too unstable to take care of him. He forms a tight bond with the boarding house's owner, whom he calls "Nanny," and she raises him as her own. Nanny's house is a haven for a diverse group of individuals in need of a fresh start—drug addicts, convicts, etc—but Nanny welcomes them in and nurtures them as they strive to become better people. Many of these boarders share their stories with Ruben, which include valuable life lessons of how they survived difficult and sometimes tragic circumstances. In doing so, they help point this young boy toward a positive and meaningful path in life.

In the movie *Akeelah and the Bee*, the main character is a precocious Black 11-year-old girl who grows up with a single mother whose primary focus is on working and simply making ends meet. After Akeelah wins her South Los Angeles middle school's spelling bee, she begins earnestly preparing for the regional one. A stern English professor who lives nearby volunteers to coach Akeelah, and with his help, she ultimately ends up a competitor at the national spelling bee in Washington, DC. Once word spreads throughout the community that Akeelah is a strong contender for the national competition, her entire community opens their hearts to her and makes time to help her prepare for success.

While the plot of each of these two movies is fictitious, they aptly exemplify the unique bond that gifted children can develop with others who nurture, encourage, and support them. These films can be inspirational for parents and children alike and are good movies to watch together as a family.

Partnering for Success

Vivien Thomas was the son of a carpenter and his grandparents were enslaved. He grew up in Nashville, Tennessee, where he graduated with honors from Pearl High School. His dream was to go to college and then medical school, but his tuition funds were lost in the great stock market crash of 1929. Instead, he became a lab technician and custodian at Vanderbilt University's medical school.

It was at Vanderbilt that Thomas met Alfred Blalock, M.D. Blalock and Thomas became friends, and under Blalock's guidance, Thomas began working in the lab continuously, performing experimental surgeries on animals and studying blood pressure and traumatic shock. Later, when Blalock became chief of surgery at Johns Hopkins University Medical School in Baltimore, he sent for Thomas to join him. It was at Johns Hopkins that Thomas and Blalock pioneered the field of heart surgery with a procedure to alleviate a congenital heart defect in newborns known as "blue baby syndrome." In 1944, with Thomas advising, Blalock successfully performed the first "blue baby" operation.

Throughout his career, Thomas was a key partner in hundreds of "blue baby" operations, advising in the operating room and performing pre- and post-operation procedures on patients. He also continued to manage Blalock's ongoing laboratory research. In addition, Thomas and Blalock taught a generation of surgeons.

In 1976, Johns Hopkins University presented Thomas with an honorary doctorate and a portrait that is still hanging in the medical school alongside that of Blalock and others. After his retirement, Thomas worked on his autobiography, *Partners of the Heart: Vivien Thomas and His Work with Alfred Blalock*, which became the basis for the PBS documentary *Something the Lord Made*. The film won many national awards and was later translated into an award-winning HBO movie (PBS: The American Experience, n.d.).

The Role of Mentors

Sometimes the people who encourage and support our children become their mentors. These individuals are typically trusted adults who are knowledgeable about and experienced in a career field that a child wishes to pursue. A mentor can help the child enhance his education and establish a strong network to assist him in advancing his career once he has finished his schooling.

One of our nation's greatest advocates for children, Marian Wright Edelman, celebrates and profiles her personal mentors in her book *Lanterns: A Memoir of Mentors* (Edelman, 2000). As a young Black girl growing up in the segregated South, then a student at Spelman College during a time when the school was a hotbed of civil rights activism, and later the first and only Black female lawyer in Mississippi, Edelman is a model of success, but she didn't do it alone. Lanterns describes the warm and loving women of Edelman's childhood community who helped raise and support her and who encouraged her to develop her talents and pursue her dreams. Edelman also credits several other people who influenced her throughout the course of her life, including such extraordinary individuals as Martin Luther King, Jr., and Robert Kennedy. Among many others, these great men inspired her to press on to promote her vision of our children as the healers of our racially-fractured society. Brief profiles of 45 "lanterns" are featured at the conclusion of the book, among them civil rights leaders, church and community members, and of course, Edelman's parents.

In similar fashion, Denzel Washington pays tribute to the people who helped him achieve success in his book *A Hand to Guide Me: Legends and Leaders Celebrate the People Who Shaped Their Lives*. In it, Washington and 75 other distinguished individuals describe the people who they remember as positively influencing the direction of their lives. The men and women (of various racial ethnicities) featured in this unique book include college administrators, medical researchers, actors, businessmen, philanthropists, political leaders, lawyers, athletes, educators, and entertainment industry leaders. Each one tells his or her own poignant story of a mentor, or "guiding hand," who provided the support and encouragement needed to succeed.

In Washington's own story, he credits his success in large part to his experiences participating in his neighborhood Boys and Girls Club. He describes the club's leaders, as well as his family and neighbors, and discusses how they all influenced and guided his development as a young boy. Today, Denzel Washington is not only a highly acclaimed actor, he also serves as a national spokesperson for the Boys and Girls Clubs of America.

Meeting the needs of students with multiple exceptionalities—3E students

Although many gifted individuals succeed because of their talents and their strengths, it is reasonable to expect that every one of them may have weaknesses as well or areas in which they many need support. Recent research on students with multiple exceptionalities recognize the challenges of students who are typically called "twice exceptional" (Kircher-Morris, 2021). When people understand their weaknesses, they can work toward overcoming them, whether by working harder in those areas or by focusing their efforts on what they're good at. Helping your child understand who she is as a learner will better equip her to make good choices and do her best work. For example, some gifted children excel at math but have weak language arts skills (reading and writing). If this is the case, your child will need to spend time working on the development of those weaker skills so that she can do well enough in school to pursue higher educational options and a career in the math-related area in which she hopes to work. Being weaker in a subject doesn't make your child less gifted; it only means that she may need to work harder at certain subjects.

Some gifted children, though strong in many areas, are also weak enough in an area that they are found to have a learning disability or other exceptional condition. Dyslexia, a type of reading difficulty, is one example of a learning disability. We have recently categorized those children as 3e-gifted, having a disability, and being culturally diverse (Davis & Robinson, 2018). A gifted child with dyslexia is still gifted and still needs a challenge, but he will also need special help in the area of his disability. Without such help, he may come to think that he is only as good as his weakest skill; he disregards his areas of strength because that work is so easy for him. As with any child, but especially for a gifted child who suffers from some type of disability, parents must be sure to emphasize their strengths. In addition, talk to your child about your own weaknesses. Discuss with him what you do well and what you cannot do well. Help him to understand that everyone has strong points and weaker ones. Accentuate the positive, and work on areas needing reinforcement.

As your child moves through school, she will likely discover areas of strength and areas in which she may need more support, whether those areas qualify as an actual weakness. If your gifted child enjoys math problems and finding solutions to number problems, for example, talk to her about math-related fields—engineering, computer science, physical sciences, banking, investments and accounting, architecture, etc. Help her learn about what people in these careers do and share information that will help her think about what she wants for her future. If at all possible, allow her to meet people in these fields. Many successful individuals are happy to talk about their careers with interested youngsters, and they may allow your child to "job shadow" for a day or so, in which your child visits them at work and observes them on the job. If a special bond is formed between the two, this adult may become a mentor for your child.

In addition to areas of strength, your child will also have areas of strong interest. If he is lucky, he will be most interested in his strength areas, although it does happen that a child may find himself interested in something that he is not particularly good at. As a parent, you can help your child to understand that not all our interests can become a career for us; sometimes we need to save our lesser talents for hobbies instead. However, if your child is driven to succeed in a particular subject, offering your support is the best thing you can do. Encourage your child to work hard and build on his successes. Teach him to use his strengths to find ways to overcome his weaker areas. Instill in him the values of discipline, effort, and a strong work ethic. He will thank you for it when he is able to succeed in his areas of passion.

The Impact of a Strong Work Ethic on Student Success

Gifted children generally try to live up to the expectations of their parents, teachers, and other important adults in their lives. They may also do the reverse—they live down to low expectations. Establishing high expectations for your children's academic achievement or talent development will likely cause them to work hard to attain their goals. Of course, setting unrealistically high expectations for their accomplishments will only frustrate them, and it may cause the opposite effect—they quit trying because they know they cannot accomplish what you want them to. However, as a parent, you must make it clear that you will not accept less than the best your child can do, but you must also be flexible and open to hear concerns that your child shares about what is happening in school. It all starts at home.

Doing one's best usually means good, honest, hard work, and practice in the area of strength. To establish a strong work ethic in your child, begin when he is young. Start with assigning household chores, ensuring that your child understands what is expected of him. You may need to monitor him, since gifted children often dislike performing tasks that they do not see as important to them or which take them away from their favor ite activities, such as reading, creating music, painting, experimenting with science, playing automated games, or building intricate structures out of Legos. Their resistance to doing basic household chores is a perfect opportunity for you as a parent to teach them that their actions and behaviors have consequences— some of which are unpleasant when they don't perform as expected. In addition, learning to complete chores at a young age will lead your child to a better understanding of responsibility later in life.

We also find that Black children are subject to stereotyping, micro-aggressions and underestimating by school personnel. Without a good relationship with your child, you may never know what your child is facing at school. Reports from families and gifted students indicate that even when students are working their hardest, they may come into contact with school personnel who underestimate their potential. Parents should be on the lookout for teachers who do not believe in their child's potential because they hold biased views of Black students in the classroom, including those who have high potential.

Gifted children often challenge rules that they don't understand or agree with, and your child may ask you for your reasoning behind specific rules. These children are also typically very persuasive, and they may try to encourage you to bend now and then. As a parent, you need to be firm and consistent in how your rules are managed. Consistency in your expectations and in your rewards and punishments is essential.

It is important for you to establish rules for your child when she is young. Once she becomes a teenager, it is very difficult to set such limits unless you have done so regularly in the past. Be strong, consistent, and hold your ground so that even the most dedicated "scientist-to-be" will clean up her room and contribute to the household as expected. This same student will then also understand the value of completing school assignments and submitting homework on time. Knowing that unpleasant tasks are simply a part of life will help her to work hard, even in subjects or at projects that hold little interest for her.

One study on the origins of motivation and talent in adolescents showed that students in positive, achievement-oriented households credited their parents' rules regarding grades and self-discipline as being very important to their achievement. Additionally, the teens in this study were found to have parents who encouraged them to seek out challenges and new opportunities to learn things that they had not yet experienced (Csiksentmihayli, Rathunde, & Whalen, 1996). Thus, setting high expectations for work that your student is expected to complete, as well as encouraging him to find new challenges to work on, will convey to your gifted child that you believe in his high potential and ability to achieve.

In a 2011 awarding-winning book, *Outliers: The Story of Success*, Malcolm Gladwell explores the factors that contribute to success by examining various groups and individuals who experienced success in their lives. Among other things, he suggests that successful people are those who have taken advantage of opportunities presented to them, those who have learned how to speak up for themselves, and, most importantly, those who know the value of hard work (Gladwell, 2011).

As a parent, you will be continuously challenged as you aim to help your gifted child build a successful future for himself as an adult. Here are some tips to help you nurture his gifts and encourage him to make the most of opportunities to reach success in any area of human endeavor:

○ Remember that no matter how gifted your child may be, she is a child first. Even intellectually bright children need parents to guide, protect, and nurture them. Although your child may talk like an adult and appear to be "wise beyond her years," she still needs you to be the parent, establishing rules and limits and providing guidance and affection. Good parenting for all children at all stages is good parenting, even with gifted children.

○ Focus on the values of hard work and effort rather than on your child's "gift." It's okay to let your child know that he is special; however, help him understand that having exceptional abilities without hard work and commitment to task will likely result in disappointment, underachievement and, sometimes, failure.

○ Encourage your child to develop personal resilience by allowing her to fail and to learn from her mistakes. For example, if your child does poorly on a school project in a subject that is difficult for her, encourage her to keep working until she achieves success. It will also benefit her to witness you "bouncing back" from a difficult challenge; talk with her and let her know how the experience affected you. Remind her of others who have overcome challenging life situations to become successful. Posting inspirational quotes in your home regarding the benefits of repeated attempts at difficult tasks might be helpful at this time.

○ Assist your child in finding a friend or group of friends who share similar interests. When gifted children find peers who think like they do and become excited about the things that they are excited about, they often seem to energize one another. This energy is easily transferred into work in the children's areas of passion.

○ Spend time with your children. Take them on educational and cultural trips to broaden their knowledge, enrich their lives, and help them begin to develop their areas of interest. This time together also shows your children that learning and discovering what they are interested in is important to you.

○ Most importantly, be a role model for your child in hard work, resilience, family values, and a love of learning. As your child's parent, you are the most significant adult in his life. If you model healthy ways to become successful, your child will follow your lead and learn to find success as well.

There are so many stories of gifted Blacks who defied the odds to achieve great things. Some of these individuals overcame hardships so severe that we may never be able to fully comprehend them, and yet they succeeded in changing the world. Your gifted child also will face challenges that seem insurmountable at times, but if our forebears were able to do it, then our children can do it, too. However, they need our guidance and support, and exposing them to as many success stories of Blacks in America as possible is a great way to keep them motivated and inspired. These stories can come from Africa, early America, or even our own families and neighborhoods. The important thing is to keep our youngsters focused on maintaining a strong sense of who they are and what they have the ability to accomplish. When children know that they are loved and supported by their families and friends, their potential for success is limitless.

Final Thoughts

My experiences as a parent, "Nana," member of a large family, scholar who has traveled around the world, and career educator have exposed me to a wealth of useful information for this book. I am confident that something here has made a difference in your understanding of who your gifted children are, how they view the world, and the multiple challenges they face daily. The resources and information provided in this book are by no means exhaustive. There are educators, parents, researchers, and other advocates working each day to add to the collection of useful tools for parents of gifted children of all cultures around the world.

I hope that reading this book is just the beginning of actions that you will find yourself engaging in on a regular basis as a parent of uniquely gifted sons and daughters. You now have what many parents are only just acquiring—information about gifted children, the special challenges they face, and educational options that may be available to them. With this knowledge, you can become an active advocate and a mentor to other parents who are less informed than you.

Remember, earlier in the book I mentioned that it was strong parent advocates who bring educators' attention to the needs of gifted children in public schools, and today it is parents who will continue to help teachers, administrators, and policy makers understand how important it is that we nurture and challenge high potential in our youth. I hope you will continue to advocate for the gifted children in your family, church, or community. Give other parents materials to read (like this book), and talk with them about what it means for a child to be gifted and what services may be available in schools for them.

Since you are now more informed about gifted learners and gifted education, you might volunteer to serve on a committee for your local or state gifted child association, or perhaps on a committee at the school. To start, you can contact your district's local coordinator of gifted programs and begin with school information meetings or PTA meetings, or you can begin organizing parents with similar concerns within your community or church. The number of parents and family members who will join you may vary. Sometimes it may be two or three; other groups start out with 20 or more. Whatever the size of the group, continue in organized efforts to distribute information, share the experiences that your children have had, and let other parents know what is available for their high-ability learners.

The role of family members, including parents, grandparents, and caretakers, is more important than that of any other individuals who come into contact with children in their lifetime. Your interactions with your children, your nurturing, and your support of them will determine how they view the world and access opportunities in it. The end result of strong parenting—characterized by sensitivity, the ability to listen, a high energy level, a solid knowledge base about resources, and most of all, a positive spirit—will be a young person whose gifts and talents are of great benefit to your family, your community, and the world.

Glossary for
Gifted Education Advocates

Ability grouping: Students are grouped by ability for instruction. This can occur in many different ways. For instance, sometimes gifted students are all placed in the same high-level classes; other times they are all placed together in the same classroom with average-ability students. Ability grouping gives advanced students the benefit of learning with academic and intellectual peers.

Ability tests: Often also referred to as intelligence tests, ability tests measure a student's general ability to succeed in a school setting. These tests sample a wide range of experiences and measure the student's ability to apply information in new and different ways.

Acceleration: An instructional option that allows gifted students to be exposed to more advanced material than what is normally taught in the regular classroom. Although there are a multitude of ways in which students can be accelerated (gifted programming expert Karen Rogers has identified at least 19 of them1), there are two basic types of acceleration:

- *Whole-grade acceleration:* skipping a grade, or entering kindergarten early

- *Single-subject acceleration:* acceleration in a subject area of strength, either by moving to a higher-level classroom just for that subject or by receiving advanced instruction within the regular class

Achievement tests: These tests assess children in specific subject areas, such as reading or mathematics, to show mastery of facts and other information learned at school or at home. Results are influenced heavily by how much opportunity a child has had to learn these subjects.

Advanced Placement (AP): AP classes are college-level classes taken in high school and taught by high school teachers for high school credit. The courses are challenging and help prepare students for college-level work. At the end of an AP course, students take a national test that could earn them college credits, depending on their score and on the policies of individual universities. Some large high schools offer 10 or more AP classes, making it possible for students who take several of these courses to enter college with a sophomore standing.

Appeal: When a decision is made that a child is not eligible for special services, parents may have the right to request that the decision be reconsidered. Many school districts have special requirements for this process, which typically including a timeframe in which the appeal must be filed. Check with the district before the eligibility committee meets to ask about the appeals process; that way, you'll know how many days after the decision is made you will have to file an appeal, as well as any other requirements you must meet to ensure that your appeal is considered.

Charter schools: Charter schools are elementary or secondary schools that receive public funding but have been released from some of the rules, regulations, and statutes that apply to other public schools.

Cluster grouping: The process of organizing students within a grade level by ability for instruction in small groups. A cluster group may be composed of three to seven or more gifted students at the elementary or middle school level who are placed within a regular classroom with their average-ability peers. Clustering allows students to learn in settings with their intellectual peers while also receiving services provided to all students.

Competitions: Contests that take place outside of school in which students compete with each other using the knowledge and skills they have learned.

Curriculum compacting: Content that the student already knows is eliminated from the curriculum, and the extra time available is spent on enrichment.

Differentiation: A gifted child is in the same classes as his age peers, but the coursework is modified for him to accommodate his special learning needs. Differentiation also may be called *individualization*. Teachers must have special training to learn how to differentiate coursework.

Dual enrollment: Students who take both high school and college courses at the same time participate in what is known as dual enrollment. This gives gifted students an opportunity to study subjects not available at their high schools. Dual enrollment requires a joint partnership between high schools and two-year or four-year colleges and universities, since these students are not able to meet normal college entrance requirements. Students then earn both high school and college credit.

Eligibility committee: The group of school officials (usually a teacher, gifted education specialist, school psychologist or counselor, and a school administrator) who meet to review all available information to determine a student's eligibility for gifted education services.

Enrichment: Curriculum is modified or extended for gifted stu dents, usually by adding material that allows them to explore related issues or work with more advanced material.

Gifted program curricula: Academic material characterized by higher-level content and/or a faster pace, with opportunities for students to select topics and projects of interest for in-depth study. Gifted education teachers have specialized training through coursework or professional development opportunities to teach the gifted education curriculum. Program models for gifted students vary widely in the amount of time and the depth of learning that gifted children spend with the more advanced curriculum.

Homeschooling: The education of children at home, typically by parents but sometimes by tutors, rather than in the formal settings of public or private schools. Once a strategy used primarily by religious communities to preserve their value systems, homeschooling is increasingly used by families of gifted children when efforts to accommodate student learning needs within the regular school seem to be falling short.

Identification: The process of discovering a person's gifted intellectual potential by reviewing results of tests, work samples, and other criteria.

Independent study: Students work one-on-one with a teacher to study a special topic of interest in depth and to accommodate the child's specific needs and learning styles.

Intelligence (IQ) tests: Tests that sample a wide range of abilities and emphasize skills such as memory and general problem-solving ability. Intelligence tests are less influenced by additional opportunities than are achievement tests.

International Baccalaureate (IB) program: The IB program is an internationally sanctioned program for middle and high school students. This program offers a comprehensive curriculum that focuses on higher-level learning skills, creative thinking, interdisciplinary studies, and community service. Students take exams in their junior and senior years, as well as write a lengthy essay and complete other requirements to be eligible for an International Baccalaureate diploma, which allows them to apply to any university in the world.

Learning contract: A student and teacher negotiate and agree to an individual learning/lesson plan in which the student is responsible for some of her own learning, checking in with the teacher at agreed-upon intervals. The contract is written and then signed by both the student and the teacher (and perhaps the parent).

Magnet schools: Public schools with specialized courses or curricula which draw students from other school zones.

Mandate: A law or directive by a local, state, or national authority to perform a certain action. The directive is usually written into regulation or code as determined by the authority of the governing body. Some states have a mandate or requirement that school districts provide services to students who are gifted and talented; however, gifted services in schools are not federally mandated.

Mentorship programs:

Students spend time observing and working with individuals in the community for a negotiated period of time to provide them with opportunities to learn advanced skills and/or to expose them to information and techniques that are not readily available at school.

Multiple criteria:

The use of several sources of data to make a decision regarding a child's eligibility for gifted services. For example, an eligibility committee might look at a child's grades, a portfolio of his best schoolwork, teacher comments, achievement test scores, and ability or intelligence test scores. Using multiple criteria provides a better opportunity for the student's exceptional potential to be considered and evaluated.

Nationally standardized tests:

Tests that are intended to be used with students across the country that have been administered to a fairly large sample of individuals (a norming group) who represent different ethnic, gender, and regional groups. The responses of the norming group provide the basis for determining the average score, as well as scores that are below or above the average.

Nomination:

The act of recommending a student for consideration for the gifted program. Parents, teachers, and other professionals may nominate students.

Online Coursework:

Students earn credit in high school or college by working from home through an online program. Many homeschooled children take advantage of distance learning for some of their classes, even earning a high school diploma while working out of a remote location.

Portfolio:	A collection of work samples completed by a student over time in different settings (home, school, or other, such as in community activities). Educators evaluate the portfolio to determine the level of the student's performance in school and in non-school-related activities.
Private and parochial schools:	Private schools are under the financial and managerial control of a private body or non-profit organization. Generally, the students must pay fees to attend. If the school engages in religious education in addition to a conventional education, it is referred to as a parochial school.
Pull-out/send-out classes:	Students leave their regular classes for one day (or part of the day) each week to participate in enrichment or extension activities.
Referral:	Similar to nomination, some school districts ask that professionals, such as teachers, counselors, and administrators refer students for services when special traits are recognized.
School-within-a-school:	All of the gifted students from a district attend the same school, along with regular students, and work in advanced classes for part of the day, spending the rest of the day mixed with the other students.
Self-contained schools for the gifted:	All students in the school are gifted in one or more areas of study.
Talent search programs:	Programs operating through several different universities across the country that identify gifted students through their strong performance on above-level standardized tests (i.e., tests originally designed for older students). These students are given the opportunity to participate in highly advanced classes in a variety of subjects—such as computer science, anthropology, or mathematics—in residential programs on certain college campuses.

Telescoping: Any technique that shortens the amount of time a student is provided to acquire content and skills. This can include acceleration or compacting, and it can be in a specific subject or across a grade level.

Mirror Books

Last Name	First Name	Book Title	Year	Genre
Abrams	Stacey	*Stacey's Extraordinary Words*	2022	picture book ages 3-8
Barnes	Derrick	*I am Everything Good*	2020	Picture Book
Barnes	Derrick	*The King of Kindergarten*	2019	Fiction
Barton	Chris	*Whoosh!!Lonnie Johnson's Super Soaking Stream of Inventions*	2016	Biography
Beaty	Andrea	*Aaron Slater, Illustrator*	2021	fiction
Beaty	Andrea	*Ada Twist, Scientist*	2016	Fiction, Picture book
Bolden	Tonya	*Searching for Sarah Rector: the Richest Black girl in America*	2014	Biographical History
Booker	Thomishia	*Brown Boy Joy*	2018	inspirational
Bowen	Natasha	*Skin of the Sea*	2021	fantasy
Brown	Tameka Fryer	*Not Done Yet: Shirley Chisholm and the Fight for Change!*	2022	Biography
Bryan	Zahra	*Black Girl Magic: A Book About Loving Yourself Just the Way You Are*	2020	inspirational
Butler	Octavia	*Kindred*	2003	Science Fiction
Bynum/ Drummond	Betty/ Joshua	*I Am A Brilliant Little Black Boy!*	2016	fiction
Celano	Marianne	*Something Happened in Our Town: A Child's Story About Racial Injustice*	2019	fiction

Last Name	First Name	Book Title	Year	Genre
Cherry	Matthew	*Hair Love*	2019	fiction
Cline-Ransome	Lesa	*Counting the Stars: The Story of Katherine Ransome, NASA Mathematician*	2019	Biography, ages 4-8
Coleman	Delanda	*What's My Superpower? Discovering Your Unique Talents*	2021	fiction
Copeland	Misty	*Black Ballerinas: My Journey to Our Legacy*	2021	Non-fiction
Crothers	Tim	*Queen of Katwe:One Girl's Triumphant Path to Becoming a Chess Champion*	2016	Biography
Davis	Sampson	*The Pact: Three young men make a promise and fulfill a dream*	2006	Biography
Dias	Hannah Carmona	*Beautiful, Wonderful, Strong Little Me!*	2019	fiction
Dias	Marley	*Marley Dias gets it done and So can you*	2018	inspirational autobiography
Diggs	Taye	*Chocolate Me*	2011	picture book/ autobiography
Favilli	Elena	*Rebel Girls: 25 Tales of Powerful Women*	2021	Biographies
Ferguson	Fabian	*Daddy's Arms*	2018	fiction
Forna	Namina	*The Gilded Ones*	2021	Fantasy, Black girl power
Gluck	Ana Cristina	*Mi Familia: A Mexican American Family*	2020	Fiction
Gorman	Amanda	*Change Sings*	2021	Lyrical Picture Book
Gorman	Amanda	*The Hill We Climb*	2021	Poetry
Hannah-Jones	Nicole & Watson, Renee	*Born on the Water- The 1619 Project*	2021	History
Harrison	Vashti	*Little Legends: Exceptional Men in Black History*	2019	Nonfiction
Harrison	Vashti	*Little Legends: Bold Women in Black History*	2017	Nonfiction
hooks	bell	*Skin Again*	2017	Picture Book

Last Name	First Name	Book Title	Year	Genre
Hudson	Cheryl Willis	*Recognize: An Anthology Amplifying & Honoring Black Life*	2021	Historical/ Inspiratonal
Hudson	Wade	*Defiant: Growing up in the Jim Crow South*	2021	a memoir
Jackson	Linda Williams	*The Lucky Ones*	2022	fiction
Johnson	Katherine	*Reaching for the Moon:The Autobiography of NASA Mathematician Katherine Johnson*	2020	autobiography
Kamkwamba	William	*The Boy who harnessed the Wind*	2016	Biography
Kapernick	Colin	*I Color Myself Differently*	2022	autobiography
Langley	Sharon	*A Ride to Remember*	2020	nonfiction
Lockington	Mariama	*For Black Girls Like Me*	2019	Inspirational
Mante	Priscilla	*The Dream Team: Jaz Saantos vs. The world*	2021	Fiction
Mbalia	Kwame	*Black Boy Joy*	2021	Compilation of stories
Mbalia	Kwame	*Last Gate of the Emperor*	2021	Future fantasy
McDaniels	Darryl (Run DMC)	*Darryl's Dream*	2022	Child's biography/inspriational
Moore	David	*The Stars Beneath Our Feet*	2019	Fiction
Mosca	Julia Finley	*The Girl with a mind for Math, the Story of Raye Montague*	2020	Biography
Muhammad	Malik	*My silent Loud: The Voice Inside Every Little Black Boy*	2019	Memoir
Myers	Walter Dean	*The Cruisers (three book series)*	2010-2012	Fiction (teen)
Neil	Alice King	*Keep your head up*	2021	Fiction-Inspirational
Nyong'o	Lupita	*Sulwe*	2019	Fiction
Perry	Jamar J	*Cameron Battle and the Hidden Kingdoms*	2022	Science Fiction/ Fantasy
Ramee'	Lisa Moore	*A Good Kind of Trouble*	2020	Fiction
Redd	Nancy	*The Real Santa*	2021	Fiction

Last Name	First Name	Book Title	Year	Genre
Reynolds	Jason	As Brave as You Are	2017	Fiction
Reynolds	Jason	Long Way Down	2019	Fiction
Ringold	Faith	Tar Beach	1996	memoir
Robinson	Shawn Anthony	Dr. Dyslexia Dude (with Guidebook for Teachers)	2019	graphic novel
Scott	Brittany	Limitless Me	2020	Inspirational
Shakur	Tupac	The Rose that Grew from Concrete	2009	Inspirational Poetry
Sherman	Charlotte Watson	Brown Sugar Babe	2020	Fiction
Shetterly	Margot Lee	Hidden Figures	2016	Hist/ Biography
Sidney	Ronnie	Nelson Beats the Odds	2015	graphic novel
Skloot	Rebecca	Henrietta Lacks	2010	Hist/ Biography
Slade	Suzanne	A Computer called Katherine: How Katherine Johnson Helped put America on the Moon	2019	biography for children
Stone	Nic	Dear Martin (2 book series)	2017	Fiction
Students	Kaufman School of Arts	Who is Florence Price?	2021	Biography
Thomas	Angie	The Hate U Give	2017	Inspirational
Thorpe	Andrea	The Story of Katherine Johnson	2021	Biography
Watson	Renee	Piecing me Together	2018	Fiction
Weatherford	Carole Boston	Schomburg:The Man who built a Library	2017	Biography
Woodard	Bellen	More than Peach	2021	Inspirational
Woodson	Jacqueline	Brown Girl Dreaming	2014	autobiography
Woodson	Jacqueline	The year we Learned to Fly	2022	inspirational
Workneh	Lilly	Good Night Stories for Rebel Girls: 100 Real-Life Tales of Black Girl Magic	2021	Non-fiction

Special Enrichment Programs for Gifted and Advanced Learners

Program	Website
Arizona Arizona State University Barrett Summer Scholars Program (for middle and high school students)	http://promise.asu.edu/bss
California Hidden Genius Project (trains & mentors Black male youth in technology, entrepreneurship, and leadership)	https://hiddengeniusproject.org/
Colorado University of Northern Colorado Young Children Program (ages four to those entering grade 4); Summer Enrichment Program (entering grades 5-10); Leadership Program (entering grades 11-12)	http:unco.edu/sep
Connecticut University of Connecticut Mentor Connection (for students entering their junior or senior year)	www.gifted.uconn.edu/mentor
Illinois Northwestern University, Center for Talent Development	www.ctd.northwestern.edu

Program	Website
Louisiana Timbuktu Academy, Southern University, Baton Rouge, Mentoring Future Scientists	www.phys.subr.edu/TA/ TAhome.htm
Louisiana University of Louisiana, Lafayette Center for Gifted Education, Daytime Enrichment Program (one-week residential program)	http://coe.louisiana.edu/ centers/ summer_prgms/ summer_pgm_info.html
Maryland Center for Talented Youth, Johns Hopkins (both onsite and online courses and programs)	http://cty.jhu.edu
Massachusetts Girls Inc., Eureka! preparing teen-age girls to participate in innovated STEM careers)	https://www.girlsincworcester. org/
Michigan Yunasa Summer Camp (for highly gifted students ages 10-14)	www.educationaladvance-ment.org/ programs/yunasa
Montana Carroll College Gifted Institute (grades 5-9)	www.carroll.edu/academics/ gifted
Nevada Davidson Institute for Talent Development	www.ditd.org
New Jersey Rutgers University, Girls in Engineering and Technology	www.osd.rutgers.edu/target
New Jersey utgers University, Young Scholars in Discrete Mathematics	http://dimacs.rutgers.edu/ysp
North Carolina UNC-Asheville Super Saturday (six-week Saturday morning pro-gram for grades 3-8)	www.unca.edu/oaci/supersat-urday

Program	Website
Tennessee Vanderbilt Programs for Talented Youth (1-3 week programs for grades 8-12); Summer Robotics Program (for grades 5-6)	www.pty.vanderbilt.edu/vsa
Virginia The College of William and Mary, Center for Gifted Education	www.cfge.wm.edu
Virginia University of Virginia Summer Enrichment Programs (grades 4-10)	www.virginia.edu/sep
Virginia Virginia Governor's Schools (for high school students), including Regional Summer Governor's School	www.doe.virginia.gov/instruc- tion/ governors_school_pro- grams/index.shtml
Wisconsin Wisconsin Center for Academically Talented Youth	www.wcaty.org
Other summer and enrichment programs can be found at: www.hoagiesgifted.org www.davidsongifted.org	

Organizations, Clubs, Advocacy Groups, and Other Resources of Interest

Resource	Contact Information
100 Black Men of America (mentoring program, specialized schools, test-taking seminars, political advocacy, scholarships, multiple programs nationwide)	www.100blackmen.org (404) 688-5100
The Black Collegian (journal)	www.blackcollegian.com
Black Issues in Higher Education (journal)	www.jbhe.com
Boys and Girls Clubs of America (academic, athletic, and mentoring programs; character and leadership programs; community centers nationwide)	www.bgca.org (404) 487-5700
Children's Defense Fund (national advocacy organization)	www.childrensdefense.org (212) 628-8787
Civil Rights Project, Harvard University (research projects and advocacy)	www.law.harvard.edu/ civilrights (617) 496-6367
Diverse Issues in Higher Education (journal)	www.diverseeducation.org

Resource	Contact Information
Education Trust (research, resources related to achievement in schools)	www.edtrust.org (800) 521-2118
Girls, Inc. (programs designed to improve girls' self esteem, leadership, character, and achievement in school; also focuses on health and empowerment)	www.girlsinc.org (212) 509-2000
Jack and Jill (leadership and service programs for ages 2-19; largest African American family organization in America)	http://national. jackandjillonline.org (202) 667-7010
National Achievers Society, Centers of Excellence (to increase the pool of students prepared for college, it hosts the annual Brain Bowl competition, with sites across the country)	www.fefonline.org (813) 272-2772
National Association of Negro Business and Professional Women's Clubs (programs, scholarships)	www.nanbpwc.org (202) 483-4206
National Black Data Processors Association/Student Programs (technology competitions, scholarships, programs)	www.bdpa.org/student-programs.php (301) 322-3434
National Child Care Information Center (advocacy, resources)	www.nccic.org (800) 616-2242
National Council of Negro Women (education, public service, and advocacy programs; sponsors the Reading Leadership Academy, National Center for African American Women, annual National Black Family Reunion, and other important programs)	www.ncnw.org (202) 737-0120

Resource	Contact Information
National Society of Black Engineers/Pre-College Initiative (science and engineering competitions; family math resources; "Math-a-lon" competition; scholarships promoting leadership, academic, and technical skills of student participants)	www.pci.nsbe.org (703) 549-2207
National Urban League (multiple programs on community involvement, educational achievement, and advocacy)	www.nul.org (212) 558-5300

Selected Books for Educators, Parents, Advocates & Equity Activists

Title (Date of Publication)	Author(s)
The Emancipation of Evan Walls (2019)	Blount, Jeffrey
Between the World & Me (2015)	Coates, Ta-Nahesi
Fugitive Pedagogy (2021)	Givens, Jarvis R.
The Short & Tragic Life of Robert Peace: A brilliant young man who left Newark for the Ivy League (2015)	Hobbs, Jeff
The Dreamkeepers: Successful Teachers of Black Children (2022)	Ladson-Billings, Gloria
We Want to do More than Survive (2019)	Love, Bettina
Cultivating Genius (2020)	Muhammad, Gholdy
The Hate U Give (2022)	Thomas, Angie
Black Fatigue: How racism erodes the body, mind & spirit (2020)	Winters, Mary-Frances
The Brilliance of Black Boys: Cultivating School success in the Early Grades (2018)	Wright, Bryan & Counsel, Shelley

A Culturally Responsive Equity-Based Bill of Rights for Gifted Children of Color

I. ADVOCACY and ACCOUNTABILITY

Gifted students of color have:

○ The right to all gifted education policies and procedures grounded in equity and inclusion

○ The right to an administrative structure committed to hiring and retaining gifted teacher of color

○ The right to be served by educators devoted to recruiting and retaining students of color in gifted education programs

○ The right to be served by educators committed to removing barriers to accessing gifted education services

○ The right to state and district policies that require educators to be formally prepared/trained in gifted education

○ The right to state and district policies that require educators to be formally trained in culturally relevant and rigorous curriculum and pedagogy

○ The right to have gifted students of color communities fully engaged with educators in collaborative advocacy processes

○ The right to a family and community advocacy group that represents their culture, background, and experiences

○ The right to an administrative structure that seeks funding for gifted programs and services in all federally funded programs —particularly Title I, II, III and IV

○ The right to a guarantee that all equity data are inclusive of opportunities, access and support within Consolidated States' plans. This includes the Every Student Succeeds Act

○ (ESSA) plans (and future legislation), as well as state level equity plans

II. ACCESS to PROGRAMMING and SERVICES

Gifted students of color have:

○ The right to participate in gifted education programs and services, including Advanced Placement, accelerated, magnet, early college, and other programs for advanced students/learners

○ The right to equitable access to gifted education programs and services

○ The right to access all district, regional and state level services that nurture their giftedness across all domains and content areas

○ The right to be served in their area(s) of gifts and talents

○ The right to access gifted and talented before school, after school, Saturday morning, and summer programs

○ The right to participate in college awareness and career development programs at institutions of higher education, including Historically Black Colleges and Universities (HBCUs)

○ The right to the development and implementation of general and gifted program policies that are equity-based

○ The right to be assessed with tools and practices that reduce and/ or eliminate bias in traditional assessment tools and practices

○ The right to be assessed for gifted education potential even if they have been referred for and served in special education (i.e., thrice exceptional—students of color who have gifted and special education needs)

○ The right to free or reduced fee gifted education programs and services

III. GIFTED PROGRAM EVALUATION and ACCOUNTABILITY

Gifted students of color have:

○ The right to district, regional, and state program assessments conducted every 3-5 years by external and culturally competent program evaluators with gifted education expertise

○ The right to annual reports to the community that reveal the "equity goal" for gifted education and all advanced programs and services

○ The right to annual equity goals and objectives for district, regional, and state programs

○ The right to teachers who engage in continuous and systematic professional learning experiences in cultural competency and multicultural education

○ The right to a program philosophy/mission/belief statement that explicitly addresses the needs of gifted students of color

IV. GIFTED EDUCATION EVALUATION and ASSESSMENT

Gifted students of color have:

○ The right to a culturally, racially, and linguistically diverse/different gifted education assessment committee

○ The right to general education, special education, pre-service, and current professionals trained and dedicated to recognizing and valuing their expressions of gifts and talents

○ The right to be evaluated and identified using multiple criteria

○ The right to be evaluated in multimodal and multi-dimensional ways

○ The right to be assessed with non-biased tests and instruments for screening and identification

○ The right to be assessed with non-verbal tests for screening and identification

○ The right to be evaluated by bilingual test examiners (e.g., school psychologists)

○ The right to be assessed by tests and instruments in their predominant or preferred language

○ The right to be assessed by tests and instruments translated into their primary or preferred language

○ The right to be assessed with culturally normed checklists

○ The right to be evaluated with tools re-normed to represent their cultural experiences and realities

○ The right to be evaluated by tests and instruments normed on students of color for screening and identification

○ The right to be assessed by tests and instructions normed locally

○ The right to educators who adhere to official testing and assessment policies and procedures

V. EDUCATORS

Gifted students of color have:

○ The right to pre-service and current educators who are unbiased and hold culturally responsive philosophies

○ The right to pre-service and current educators who are committed to becoming culturally competent

○ The right to pre-service and current educators who are committed to gifted education

○ The right for pre-service and current educators to be trained in multicultural education and gifted education

○ The right to a racially diverse/different pre-service and current gifted education teaching force

○ The right to have access to pre-service and current educators of color and members of their community who represent and can advocate for their interests, needs, and potential

○ The right to pre-service and current educators who have bilingual training and credentials

VI. CURRICULUM and INSTRUCTION

Gifted students of color have:

○ The right to culturally relevant curriculum and instruction

○ The right to authentic and multicultural content in all content areas

○ The right to rigorous multicultural curriculum and materials that reflect their cultural, racial, and linguistic background and heritage

○ The right to rigorous and authentic multicultural literature reflective of all cultures

○ The right to curricula that promotes cultural, racial, and linguistic pride

○ The right to their views being encouraged and honored rather than silenced

○ The right to curricula that will prepare them to be globally competitive and knowledgeable of world cultures

○ The right to program experiences that allow international travel and virtual engagement with their peers around the world

VII. SOCIAL and EMOTIONAL

Gifted students of color have:

○ The right to supportive services and programs by school counselors trained in multicultural counseling (theories, methods, strategies)

○ The right to counselors familiar with and skilled in racial identity theories

○ The right to counselors who understand and promote racial identity development

○ The right to counselors and teachers who understand the unique challenges of being a gifted student of color

○ The right to pre-service educators, current educators and counselors formally trained in the socio-emotional needs of gifted children of color

○ The right to counselors who understand the relationship between racial identity and achievement

○ The right to interact and be educated with peers from similar cultural, racial, and linguistic backgrounds

○ The right to academic support when they underachieve, fail, and/or make mistakes

○ The right to understand the area(s) in which they are gifted and talented

○ The right to be taught how to self-advocate to increase their access to appropriate instructional and support services

VIII. FAMILIES and COMMUNITIES

Gifted students of color have:

○ The right to educators who value the importance of their families feeling welcome in schools

○ The right to educators who collaborate with their families and communities

○ The right to educators who provide professional development to families to strengthen advocacy for their children

○ The right to have community leaders (e.g., faith leaders, community center leaders) who know and understand them in different contexts involved in the referral, identification and service delivery process

○ The right to have their families assist others in the community with understanding the benefits of gifted education programs and services

○ The right to have their families serve as 'cultural agents' to inform educators and mediate the cultural mismatch that exists between their communities and dominant culture school personnel

○ The right for schools to recruit and engage members of their communities who have been successful to serve in the critical role of mentoring

○ The right for administrative structures to respect the norms, traditions and culture of communities of color when planning and conducting events

Ford, D. Y., Dickson, K. T., Davis, J. L., Scott, M. T., & Grantham, T. C. (2018). *A Culturally Responsive Equity-Based Bill of Rights for Gifted Students of Color. Gifted Child Today*, 41(3), 125–129. https://doi.org/10.1177/1076217518769698(Ford, Dickson, Davis, Grantham, Moore & Floyd, 2020)

References

Andersen, L (2014) Visual–Spatial Ability: Important in STEM, Ignored in Gifted Education. *Roeper Review*. 36. 114-121. 10.1080/02783193.2014.884198.

Anderson, B. N. (2020). "See Me, See Us": Understanding the Intersections and Continued Marginalization of Adolescent Gifted Black Girls in U.S. Classrooms. *Gifted Child Today*, 43(2), 86–100. https://doi.org/10.1177/1076217519898216

Arrington, E. G., Hall, D. M., & Stevenson, H. C. (2003). The success of African-American students in independent schools. *Independent School*, 62(4), 10–21.

Baytops, A. (2009). Writing 'read-aloud' books: Lesson for a middle school English/Language arts class. Unpublished manuscript.

Canady H. G. (1936). The effect of "rapport" on the I. Q.: a new approach to the problem of racial psychology. *Journal of Negro Education*, 5, 209–219.

Coleman, M.R., Collins, K.H., Grantham, T.C., & Biddle, W.H. (2022). Underrepresentation in Gifted and Talented Education. In Farmer, T.W., Talbott, E., McMaster, K., Lee, D., & Aceves, T.C. (Eds.). *Handbook of Special Education Research, Volume I: Theory, Methods, and Developmental Processes* (1st ed.). Routledge. https://doi.org/10.4324/9781003156857

Copur-Gencturk, Y., Robinson-Cimpian, J., Lubienski, S., & Thacker, I. (2019). Teachers' Bias Against the Mathematical Ability of Female, Black and Hispanic Students. *Educational Researcher*. 49. 10.3102/0013189X19890577

Cotton, C.R.B., Davis, J.L., & K.H. Collins, (2002). See me! Recognizing and addressing the invisibility of gifted Black girls with other learning exceptionalities. In F.H.R., Piske, K.H. Collins & K.B. Arnstein (Eds). Critical Issues in Servicing Twice Exceptional Students: Socially, Emotionally, and Culturally Framing Learning Exceptionalities. Springer.

Csikszentmihalyi, M. (2013). *Flow: The psychology of optimal experience.* New York, NY: Random House.

Davis, J.L. (2007). An exploration of the impact of family on the achievement of African American gifted learners originating from low -income environments. Dissertations, Theses, and Masters Projects. William & Mary. Paper 1539618445. https://dx.doi.org/doi:10.25774/w4-xbgp-gn43

Davis, J.L. (2013). Martin D. Jenkins: A Voice to Be Heard. In A. Robinson & J. Jolly (Eds.) *A Century of Contributions to Gifted Education: Illuminating Lives- Key Figures in Gifted Education.* Routledge Books.

Davis, J.L. and Moore, J.L. (2016). (Eds). *Gifted Children of Color Around the World: Diverse needs, Exemplary Practices, and Directions for the Future* - Advances in Race and Ethnicity in Education. Volume 3 2016. United Kingdom: Emerald Group Publishing Limited.

Davis, J.L. & Robinson, S.A. (2018). Being 3e, a new look at culturally diverse gifted learners with exceptional conditions: an examination of the issues and solutions for educators and families. In S.B. Kaufman (Ed.), *Twice Exceptional: Supporting and Educating Bright, Creative Children with Learning Disabilities (pp.278-289).* Oxford University Press.

Davis, J.L & Goudelock, J.L. (2020, Fall). *Discussing racism with gifted children: A primer. Parenting for High Potential.* A publication of the National Association for Gifted Children. Washington, D.C.

Davis, J. L. & Douglas, D. (2021). *Empowering Underrepresented Gifted Students: Perspectives from the Field.* Free Spirit.

Davis, J.L. & Cotton, C.R.B. (2021). I'm Gifted Too: Using Culturally Responsive Teaching to address the learning needs of 3E students. *Variations Magazine.*

Davis, S., Jenkins, G., Hunt, R., & Page, L.F. (2003*). The Pact: Three Young Make a Promise and fulfill a Dream.* Penquin Books.

Daley, J. (2006). (Ed). *Great Speeches by African Americans.* Dover.

Du Bois, W.E.B. (1903). The talented tenth. In B.T. Washington (Ed.). *The Negro problem: A series of articles by representative American Negroes of today.* (pp. 31-76). James Potts & Co.

Edelman,M.R. (1999). *Lanterns: A memoir of mentors.* Beacon Press.

Edmin, C. (2017). *For White Folks Who Teach in the Hood... and the Rest of Y'all Too: Reality Pedagogy and Urban Education* (Race, Education, and Democracy). Beacon Press.

Ferguson, R. (2007). *Toward Excellence with Equity: An emerging vision for closing the achievement gap.* Cambridge, MA: Harvard Education Press.

Ford, D.Y. (2014). Segregation and the underrepresentation of Blacks and Hispanics in gifted education: Social inequality and deficit paradigms. *Roeper Review, 36,* 143-154.

Ford, D.Y., Davis, J.L., Trotman-Scott, M.F. & Sealey-Ruiz, Y. (2016). (Eds). *Gumbo: Liberating Memoirs and Stories to Inspire Females of color.* IA Publishing.

Ford, D. Y., Walters, N. M., Byrd, J. A., & Harris, B. N. (2019). I Want to Read About Me: Engaging and Empowering Gifted Black Girls Using Multicultural Literature and Bibliotherapy. *Gifted Child Today, 42*(1), 53–57. https://doi.org/10.1177/1076217518804851

Ford, D. Y., Dickson, K., Davis, J.L., Grantham, T.C., Moore, J.L., & Floyd, E. F. (2020) Equity based Culturally responsive bill of rights for gifted children of color. *Gifted Child Today.*

Gagne, F. (2003). Transforming gifts into talents: The DMGT as a development theory. In N. Colangelo & G.A. Davis (Eds.) *Handbook of gifted education* (3rd ed., pp 60-74). Allyn & Bacon.

Gailbraith, J. & Delisle, J. (2022). *The Gifted Teen Survival Guide : Smart, Sharp & Ready for Almost Anything* (5th Ed). Free Spirit Publishing.

Gladwell, M. (2011). *Outliers: The Story of Success.* Back Bay Books.

Grissom, J. A., & Redding, C. (2016). Discretion and Disproportionality: Explaining the Underrepresentation of High-Achieving Students of Color in Gifted Programs. *AERA Open, 2*(1). https://doi.org/10.1177/2332858415622175

Haight, W. L. (2001). *African American children and church: A Sociocultural Perspective.* Cambridge University Press.

Institute for Learning (2013, August) 11 Ways to teach academic skills to visual-spatial learners. http://www.institute4learning. com/2013/08/15/11-ways-to-teach-academic-skills-to-visual-spatial-learners/

Jenkins, M. D. (1936). A socio-psychological study of negro children of superior intelligence. *Journal of Negro Education,* 5, 175–190. https://doi.org/10.2307/2292155

Kircher-Morris, E. (2021). *Teaching Twice-Exceptional Learners in Today's Classrooms.* Free Spirit.

Konuru, V. (2021). Student Voices: The power of self-advocacy. In J.L. Davis & D. Douglas. *Empowering Underrepresented Gifted Students: Perspectives from the Field.* Free Spirit Publishing.

Lewis, D.L. (1993). *W.E.B. Du Bois. Vol. 1: Biography of a race. 1868-1919.* Henry Holt.

National Association of Gifted Children, n/d

New York Times (2007, Dec). For Struggling Black College, Hopes of a Revival. Laura Beil. https://www.nytimes.com/2007/12/05/education/05wiley.html

New York Times (2020). How George Floyd was killed in police custody. By Evan Hill, Ainara Tiefenthäler, Christiaan Triebert, Drew Jordan, Haley Willis and Robin Stein https://www.nytimes.com/2020/05/31/us/george-floyd-investigation.html

Nicholson-Crotty, S., Grissom, J.A., Nicholson-Crotty, J., & Redding, C. (2016). Disentangling the Causal Mechanisms of Representative Bureaucracy: Evidence From Assignment of Students to Gifted Programs. *Journal of Public Administration Research and Theory,* 26, 4, p. 745–757, https://doi.org/10.1093/jopart/muw024

Obama, B. (2006). *The Audacity of Hope: Thoughts on Reclaiming the American Dream.* Crown.

Olenchak, R. (2002). *Being a gifted boy: What have we learned?* Retrieved June 27, 2010, from www.dukegiftedletter.com/articles/vol2no4_feature.html

Piechowski, M. M. (2006). *Mellow Out, They Say, If I only Could: Intensities and Sensitivities of the Young & Bright.* Yunasa Books.

Rimm, S. (2008). *Why bright kids get poor grades and what you can do about it.* SCB Distributors.

Robinson, S.A. & Davis, J.L. (2018). From pain to the promise: Strategies for Supporting Gifted African American males with dyslexia. In D.A. Conrad & S.N.J. Blackman (Eds.) *Responding to Learner Diversity and Learning Difficulties* (pp. 77-92). Charlotte, NC: Information Age Publishing.

Ruf, D. (2009). *5 Levels of Gifted: School Issues and Educational Options.* Gifted Unlimited.

Schroth, S., Watson-Thompson, C., Davis, J.L. (2022, March). Children's literature especially appropriate for diverse gifted children. 11, 1. *Parenting for High Potential,* a publication of the National Association for Gifted Children.

Stinson, D.W.(2010). When the burden of acting White is not a burden: School success and African American male students. Www.springerlink.com/content/9140h2vg80034338

Sue, D. W. & Spanierman, L. (2020). Microaggressions in Everyday Life (2nd Ed). Wiley.

Unleashmonday.com (2022). Overexcitabilities can change your life: Meet Chris Wells https://unleashmonday.com/episodes/033

Utley, O. (2008). *Keeping the Tradition of African Storytelling Alive.* Yale University.

Witty, P.A., & Jenkins, M.D. (1935). The Case of "B"—A Gifted Negro Girl. *Journal of Social Psychology,* 6, 117-124.

Yi, S. and Gentry, M. (2021). Academic perfectionism of high-ability and high-achieving students in mathematics and science: Differential relations by identification criteria of giftedness. *Roeper Review* 43(3), 173–186.

About the Author

Joy Lawson Davis, Ed.D.'s career as an educator began more than 40 years ago as an elementary art teacher; she later served as District Coordinator of Gifted Services in three school divisions and held a five-year term as the State Specialist for Gifted Services in Virginia. In Virginia, she worked to improve gifted services statewide for underrepresented gifted students. She developed the program model and served as the first Executive Director of the Appomattox Regional Governor's School for the Arts and Technology in Petersburg, Virginia.

Davis is also currently serving on the Board of Trustees of The Roeper School of Michigan. As a highly sought out education consultant, she has provided extensive services to school districts and organizations in the United States, Trinidad, Tobago, South Africa, and the Middle East. She has authored and co-authored numerous articles and book chapters, with her primary focus being improved equity and access to gifted programs for Black and other underrepresented groups. Davis is also author of five books, including the award winning: *Bright, Talented & Black: A guide for families of African American Gifted Learners*; *Culturally Responsive Gifted Education: Building Cultural Competence and Serving Diverse Populations*; and most recently *Empowering Underrepresented Gifted Students: Perspectives from the Field*.

As a first-generation college graduate, and parent of three adult gifted individuals, Davis knows all too well the importance of a strong family support system in enabling gifted learners to reach their educational and lifetime goals. She has devoted her career to helping families and educators better understand the academic and social-emotional needs of gifted learners, particularly those who are often overlooked and thus underserved in school programs around the world. Davis is married, has three adult children, and shares seven grandchildren with her husband.

CPSIA information can be obtained
at www.ICGtesting.com
Printed in the USA
JSHW030242181222
35067JS00002B/7

9 781953 360069